Paradigm Shift:
Change Your Mindset and Live the Life of Your Dreams

D1737031

Itayi Garande

DEAN
THOMPSON
Publishing

London . New York . Harare . Johannesburg

Paradigm Shift: Change Your Mindset and Live the Life of Your Dreams

First published in Great Britain by Dean Thompson Publishing, 2023

A CIP catalogue record for this book is available from the British Library

ISBN: 9798396474147

This book is dedicated to my late father and mother, my wife and children, my late brothers, my sisters and my nieces and nephews. A special dedication to Farai 'Shifty' Bvumbe, rest in peace nephew. Till we meet again!

To my relatives, friends, colleagues, acquaintances and readers around the world, I hope this book will inspire you to have a paradigm shift, pursue your dreams relentlessly and live your dream life.

I love you all.

Itayi Garande

ALSO BY ITAYI GARANDE

*Reconditioning: Change your life in one minute**

*Shattered Heart: Overcoming Death, Loss, Breakup and Separation**

*Broken Families: How To Get Rid of Toxic People and Live A purposeful Life**

*All Amazon No. I bestsellers

TABLE OF CONTENTS

Prologue: Think Different. Be Different. Think for yourself. Be
              Yourself.   iii
Chapter 1:   What Is A Paradigm Shift?   1
Chapter 2:   Finding Purpose In Pain   9
Chapter 3:   Seize the Moment   16
Chapter 4:   Confront Your Fears   23
Chapter 5:   Discipline Your Thinking   29
Chapter 6:   Nurture Your Hunger for Success   35
Chapter 7:   The Power of Incremental Progress   41
Chapter 8:   Harness Your Creative Energy   44
Chapter 9:   Unleash Creativity with Your Subconscious Mind   49
Chapter 10:   Ignite Purpose with Passion   55
Chapter 11:   Embrace the Power of Possibility   61
Chapter 12:   The Perfect Time Is Now   69
Chapter 13:   The Power of Momentum   76
Chapter 14:   Fear Is a Great Motivator   82
Chapter 15:   Love and Paradigm Shift   90
Chapter 16:   Changing Your Mindset   95
Chapter 17:   Building Positive Habits   101
Chapter 18:   Finding Your Purpose   107
Chapter 19:   Emotional Banking   114
Chapter 20:   Whatever You Mismanage You Lose   121
Chapter 21:   Never Too Late To Change Your Paradigm   126
Chapter 22:   Flawed Paradigms Lead To Flawed Decisions   131
Chapter 23:   The Power of Perception   136
Chapter 24:   Sheer Determination and Belief in Oneself   143
Chapter 25:   The Beauty of Our Choices   155
Chapter 26:   Overcome Limiting Beliefs & Create Wealth   157
Chapter 27:   Unlock Infinite Potential   164
Chapter 28:   Epilogue: Shift That Paradigm   169

PROLOGUE

THINK DIFFERENT. BE DIFFERENT. THINK FOR YOURSELF. BE YOURSELF.

I recall a conversation with my father many years ago. I had just come home from school, a young boy of eight or nine, filled with excitement. My father, as a loving parent, was curious to know what had sparked my excitement. He asked me, "What are you so excited about?" I replied, "I heard something really nice today." Intrigued, my father eagerly inquired, "What did you hear?" I shared with him the words that I had heard from my teacher, "You were born an original, don't become a copy."

Before his passing, my father asked me, "Do you remember that day when you came home from school excited?" Surprisingly, I couldn't recall the specifics, but my father vividly remembered. So, he continued, "What happened with you? Did you become an original or a copy? What did you become?" I could not answer this question, but it got me thinking.

One of the most powerful but also tragic poems that I ever read as a child is "The Voiceless" by Oliver Wendell Holmes (1809-1894), an American physician, poet and essayist. He writes, "Alas, to those that die with their songs still inside them." Every single person on this earth has a unique song, a unique voice to express something that only they can express.

However, we live in a world where we're pressured to conform. We all want to belong and be accepted, so other people's voices, opinions, expectations and demands shape us. We do not become original.

So, the question arises: Are you an original or a copy of someone else, willingly or unwillingly, consciously or unconsciously?

It's not an easy question to answer because we'd like to think that we are being ourselves, being original and unique. Early impressions and influences in our formative years shape us to the point where we may not even know if we're following our own programme or someone else's.

To create a balance, we must understand and learn from the influences that have shaped our lives without letting them define us. We need to have deep roots, connections and good influences, but they shouldn't limit our ability to be ourselves. It takes courage to find your own voice and sing your song. By tuning in to your thoughts, feelings and desires, you can gain insight into your authentic self and what truly resonates with you.

If you think about it, it is perhaps the greatest tragedy for a person at the end of their life to be unable to say, "I truly sang my song." On the other hand, what greater joy is there than being able to say, "I did sing my song, one that inspired me and many others"?

Now, just as I am using the analogy of music, this does not mean that I'm undermining other people's influences in our lives. Instead, think of music with its different notes, each one unique, or a symphony with different musicians playing different instruments. They all join together in harmony, with each one needed and complementing the other. Similarly, think of the human body or nature—a healthy organism made up of trillions of cells and diverse systems that work together in coordination. If they all became clones of each other, it would be destructive. The paradox lies in embracing individuality while fostering harmony within diversity.

The individuality I am describing here is not an ego trip or a control game. It is simply the humble expression of oneself. At the same time, it is important to recognise how others can support and complement you without becoming them or vice versa. Jewish religious leader and scholar who lived during the 1st century BCE and 1st century CE, Hillel the Elder put it very well, "If I am I because you are you and you are you because I am I, then I am not and you are not. But if I am I because I am I and you are you because you are you, then I am and you are."

In essence, Hillel's saying highlights the significance of self-identity and personal authenticity. It suggests that one should not define their identity solely based on how others perceive them, but rather by having a genuine understanding of oneself. Additionally, it emphasises the importance of recognising and respecting the individuality of others.

In simple terms, if my identity is defined by being in juxtaposition to yours, I need to know where you are before I can find myself. Likewise, you need to define yourself by knowing where I am. In this scenario, the blind leads the blind and we will never find our identities. However, if I am I because my identity is generated from within me and you are you because your identity is generated from within you, then we can come together.

When you meet people who are comfortable in their own skin and secure, coexistence comes naturally. They don't need to fight for their turf or take anything from you to become bigger. They understand that being right doesn't require making others wrong. They help you learn how to be confident in your own right, making them the best teachers and mentors. They won't impose their opinions on you, even if they have strong ones or if you want to hear them. Instead, they will help you develop your own opinion and teach you how to think.

These individuals demonstrate restraint by allowing you to answer questions and develop your own tools and methodologies. They serve as indicators and methods for discovering your inner voice. If you have already found your inner voice, that's wonderful! May you continue to express it and teach others how to find their own voices.

However, we must also acknowledge the forces at work that often lead to lives of quiet desperation. The pressures of existence can turn routines into habits and habits into principles that are difficult to break free from. Yet, the human spirit is about the ability to break out of those patterns. That is why music has become such a powerhouse in our generation. It offers a form of escape and free-spiritedness amidst the routines, boredom and monotony of life. Music lifts our spirits and transports us to another time and place, even if only for a short while.

But the key is not just to listen to music; it is to create music and be your own music. Sing your song—the songs of your soul. Surround yourself with people who appreciate and support your unique expression. Be with those who do not try to make you sing their song or be a mere accessory or support to them. Instead, be in the company of individuals who encourage you to be true to yourself and embrace your own creative voice.

Michelangelo, an Italian artist of the High Renaissance period, said this when he was asked how he carved beautiful angels in marble, "I see the angel trapped in the marble. I carved and carved and set her free." But for that, we need effort, we need work to get out of the status quo, remove the excess and discover those engraved letters etched deep into our souls. It's not superimposing, you're just removing the blockages, the impediments and the obstacles.

But how do we remove the blockages, the impediments and the obstacles? We do this by having a paradigm shift. This is my aim with this book.

Chapter 1 - What Is A Paradigm Shift?

What you think is working against you is working for you. .

Look for the lesson in the darkness rather than curse it.

Have faith in the power of your emotions. If you sense it, it is valid. Remember you have the power to direct your mind to what you want to achieve.

Today, right now, you can decide in your heart to see a vision no one else can see; you can immediately change your way of thinking, that changes your actions and you can immediately go to a place where you could have never hoped or imagined because you chose a new paradigm.

As human beings, we often find ourselves stuck in the same old routine, doing the same things and expecting different results. But what if I told you that there is a way to break out of this cycle and create real change in your life? What if I told you that a simple mental switch can change your entire life and you can be that one person who changes your family's fortune? This is where the concept of a paradigm shift comes into play.

We all have dreams, but we do not achieve them because we use the same set of thinking tools as we've always used to try and achieve them. Unless we change the thinking tools, our dreams will never be achieved. This is the only reason why we do not achieve our dreams. Nothing else. It is important to realise that the greater the diversion from our old limiting beliefs, the greater the progression towards our goals.

You were given your dreams for the purpose of accomplishing them. That dream you are holding in your mind today is possible. Sometimes we fail to say, "I can do that." We convince ourselves that we are not enough; that we are not adequate or capable because we look at our problems and our challenges and wallow in self-pity.

Many of us simply sail through life. We are born, have relationships, work and die. We live a life with no special kind of meaning because we listen to other people's opinion of us and fail to realise our dreams.

Someone's opinion of you doesn't have to be your reality. Check yourself and stop being a doubter. Many people are living their present life on an old timeline, that's why they are vibrating low. They fail to realise that there are multiple timelines in the world and if you live someone else's timeline, you're headed for doom. You need to get off the old timeline and not let that inner victim take a hold of you.

In the process of working on your dream, you are going to encounter a lot of disappointments, failure, pain, setbacks and defeats. But in the process of doing that, you will discover some things about yourself that you don't know right now. What you will realise is that you have greatness within you and that you are more powerful than you can ever imagine. I can tell you right now, what you think is working against you is working for you.

When we first set out to pursue our dreams, we often have a clear vision of what we want to achieve. We picture ourselves succeeding, reaching our goals and living the life of our dreams. But what we don't always anticipate are the challenges that we will inevitably face along the way. These challenges can be painful and discouraging and they can make us question whether we have what it takes to achieve our goals. They can cut off the flow of our radiance and make us quit.

But it is precisely in these moments of difficulty that we have the opportunity to discover something extraordinary within ourselves. We have the chance to tap into a reservoir of inner strength and resilience that we didn't even know existed.

In these moments, we begin to see that we are capable of far more than we ever imagined. We begin to understand that we have within us a seed of greatness, waiting to be cultivated and nurtured.

This is what's called a paradigm shift.

A paradigm shift is a long-lasting change in the way we think about our lives. It's a shift in our perception of reality, a change in our beliefs and assumptions and a new way of looking at the world around us. This shift can be both personal and societal and it can have a profound impact on our lives.

A paradigm shift is not the same as a small change. A small change is a minor adjustment in our behaviour or habits, while a paradigm shift is a complete overhaul of our way of thinking and acting. A small change may lead to temporary improvements, but it won't have the same long-term impact as a paradigm shift.

Making big changes in our lives requires us to break out of our comfort zone and take risks. It requires us to challenge our beliefs and assumptions and to look at things from a different perspective. It requires us to get rid of certain beliefs, certain people, certain situations and certain habits. By completely changing our perception of reality and adopting a new way of thinking, we can overcome our fears and limitations and achieve our goals.

While a paradigm shift may seem like a daunting task, it's important to remember that it doesn't happen overnight. Instead, it's a gradual process that requires patience and persistence. One way to start making tiny steps towards a paradigm shift is to identify the areas of your life that you want to change and then set small, achievable goals.

For example, if you want to become more confident in social situations, you could start by practicing small talk with strangers. If you want to become more physically fit, you could start by walking for 10 minutes a day and gradually increasing your time and distance.

The key is to take action and make small changes every day. Over time, these tiny steps will add up and you'll start to see the results of your efforts. And before you know it, you'll have made a paradigm shift and created real change in your life.

Now that you have a better understanding of a paradigm shift and its potential to transform your life, it's time to take action.

But how do you actually make a paradigm shift happen?

This is what this book is about. The following chapters will guide you through the process of creating a paradigm shift in your life. You'll learn how to shift your mindset, break free from limiting beliefs and take action towards your goals.

Throughout the book, you'll find personal anecdotes and stories from high achievers and individuals who overcame adversity to achieve great things. These stories will inspire and motivate you, showing you that a paradigm shift is possible no matter where you come from or what obstacles you face.

Remember, creating a paradigm shift takes time and effort. It's not a one-time event, but rather an ongoing process of growth and transformation, a series of atomic habits that come together to create a completely transformed mind. The key is to take action and make small changes every day. Over time, these tiny steps will add up and you'll start to see the results of your efforts. And before you know it, you'll have made a paradigm shift and created real change in your life.

But remember. You cannot make a paradigm shift without faith, without trust. I'm talking about non-religious faith - faith that you can do it. Faith that you are capable of change. Faith that you are worthy of change.

The other thing that will hinder you is trust. Trust is a big issue, a huge issue. The question "Who can I trust?" is the most important question we ask in our lives. Have we been let down by one another? Yes, absolutely. All of us have been let down by people. Have we let ourselves down? Yes. Have our families let us down? Yes. Has your spouse, boyfriend or girlfriend let you down? Yes.

But what do we have to do? What we have to do is be willing to get up every morning and still choose to trust, regardless of our previous experience. We have to trust the schools where we send our children, the restaurants at which we eat, the people that tell us that they love us, or the companies that we work for.

We have to trust people in the hospital, working in medical care, people running companies.

We have to stop running around saying, "Oh, I don't trust anyone. I've been hurt many times." Trusting after being hurt is hard. It takes a paradigm shift. And many of us have a paradigm that says, "I won't trust people and I won't trust organisations and I certainly won't believe."

If this is your paradigm, you're sacrificing a great future.

So, if you're ready to transform your life and create a brighter future, let's get started. The journey begins now.

Bonus poem

A paradigm shift, a wondrous thing,
When old ways crumble and new ones spring,
A transformation of thought and belief,
A seismic shift, a profound relief.

It comes when we question what we know,
And let go of what we thought was so,
A shift in perspective, a change of view,
A chance to start anew.

It's not always easy, this paradigm shift,
As old beliefs may cause a rift,
But if we embrace the change with grace,

A new world may take its place.

So don't fear the shift, embrace it true,
A whole new world waits for you.

Chapter 2 – Finding Purpose in Pain

When life seems bleak and pain consumes your every thought, it's easy to lose sight of your purpose. But it's in these darkest moments that we can find the strength to rise above our struggles and discover our true calling.

Pain is not a curse, but a teacher. It shapes us, moulds us and forces us to confront our deepest fears. It teaches us resilience, empathy and the courage to stand up and fight for what we believe in..

A paradigm shift can occur when we go through difficult times. Our previous way of thinking and understanding may no longer serve us and we are forced to see things in a new light. This can be a painful process, but it can also be an opportunity for growth and transformation. By embracing the new perspective that comes with a paradigm shift, we can learn to see the purpose and meaning in our struggles, even if we couldn't see it before.

We may also develop a greater sense of empathy and compassion for others who are going through difficult times, as we have experienced it ourselves. Ultimately, a paradigm shift can help us to live more fully and authentically, as we let go of old beliefs and embrace a new way of being in the world.

Everyone experiences crushing pain in their lives, regardless of who they are. We all go through seasons of death, desperation and disappointment. Dreams can be shattered, relationships can crumble and businesses can fail. It can feel like everything is falling apart. But it's often through these difficult experiences that we gain wisdom that we can't find anywhere else: wisdom that forces us to have a paradigm shift.

When we're going through trials, it's tempting to look at our lives with a perspective of pain. But there's a purpose in your pain. Holocaust survivor, Viktor E. Frankl, in his renowned book, *Man's Search for Meaning*, Frankl reflects on his experiences in Nazi concentration camps and explores the importance of finding meaning in life, even in the midst of unimaginable suffering. Frankl says you're being prepared for something far greater through the trials, struggles and pain you're experiencing now.

He was in a spiritual warfare that he eventually won. The pain that he was feeling at the time could not compare to the joy that was coming. He could not see it at the time.

Regarding the purpose of pain, Frankl's perspective today is that while we cannot always control or avoid pain and suffering, we can choose how we respond to it. He suggests that by finding meaning in our suffering, we can transform it into a source of growth and resilience. He believed that even in the face of extreme adversity, individuals have the freedom to choose their attitude and response and this can give their pain a sense of purpose.

When he was on his deathbed, Frankl found his *death motivation*. He was unafraid to die. He said, "Humans don't want to die because deep in their hearts they know that they have not finished what they were born to start. That's why they don't want to die. I discovered my purpose and I am ready to die."

When a person has discovered their purpose and fulfilled their destiny, they welcome death. Death never threatens a human who discovers their purpose.

In *The Power of Now: A Guide to Spiritual Enlightenment*, Eckhart Tolle discusses the purpose of pain through his concept of the "pain-body," a collection of accumulated emotional pain from past experiences. The *pain-body* can be triggered in the present, leading to emotional reactions that continue the cycle of suffering. However, by becoming aware of the *pain-body* and accepting it without resistance, individuals can gradually dissolve its grip and find liberation from its influence.

Tolle suggests that suffering, however, can deepen one's spiritual journey by prompting self-inquiry and the search for a higher truth. It can motivate individuals to seek a deeper understanding of themselves and their existence, leading to spiritual growth and transformation.

Nelson Mandela is an example of someone who endured great suffering, spending years in prison for a crime he didn't commit. But it was through his time in prison that he gained the wisdom and strength to become the president of South Africa. If he hadn't endured the prison, he might never have become president. His difficult experiences in life created further opportunities for growth and success.

Don't think that your life is just random. Mandela's life was not random. It was someone's great escape. What does that mean? It means that the pain, the things that he experienced in his life, were not just for him. There was a greater purpose. He had become the "one" for the "we". He had to overcome so that he could reach back and help others.

We are sometimes "crushed" in the most unexpected ways. The seed can't think or understand the suffering it endures when it gets buried, but that "burial" is necessary for growth. It doesn't know what the veterinarian is doing; it just has to trust him, constricting himself to his methods. If we're going through a difficult time right now, it might be hard to see the purpose behind our pain. But it's important to remember that we can find meaning and purpose in even the most difficult experiences.

I didn't wake up the person you see today, not by a long shot, nowhere close. If you had met me at 18 and told me that I would end up being an author of four books, a lawyer, a multiple property owner, I would have laughed in your face. Even if I had told my neighbours and my classmates that I would travel the globe, they would have laughed at me. I was a simple little boy, but I didn't know what was in store for me. I thought I was going to be a singer, but little by little, step by step, day by day, situation by situation, I was moving towards my purpose and destiny, not only by the doors that opened but also by the doors that closed.

I come from humble beginnings and responded too much to ancestry and parents' trauma. Recent studies in epigenetics tell us that we can change our bloodline; we can shift our paradigm and create success even if our ancestors never did and even if our parents experienced a lot of trauma.

In spite of my upbringing, I didn't know what was in the making, but it was necessary that I come from there because of the heights I would go. I couldn't go lower. The bow had to be pulled way back for my arrow to go far.

I have written books that have been number one bestsellers and have been translated into multiple languages around the world, with *Reconditioning: Change Your Life In One Minute* being translated into four different languages. I can't read the Swahili and Mandarin translations, but I trust those who professionally translated them for me.

All these things would come out of a guy who was just writing short stories in the seventh grade and running around barefoot playing in mud puddles. I didn't know what was in the making while I was aching, crying, or suffering, but I was moving towards my destiny.

I was seeking answers when my mother had a heart attack or when my father died, but no one could explain why it happened. Even when I prayed to have my mother saved, no one answered. It was then that I realised that it's dangerous to seek answers while suffering, as it can lead to frustration and distraction. Sometimes, you just have to settle to walk in the dark and walk by faith, not by sight, then you can have that paradigm shift.

My pain at the time was some sort of pruning. Pruning is not punishment and suffering does not mean you are cursed or being punished. Pruning is how we realise that we are valuable because we wouldn't be pruned if we were a dying bush. Nobody prunes a dead bush, only a fruitful one. That realisation for me was a paradigm shift.

Bonus poem

In the midst of anguish and despair,
When pain seems like too much to bear,
We often search for meaning and reason,
A purpose to our suffering, in any season.

For in the depths of our darkest hours,
Our pain can give way to greater powers,
It can teach us lessons we never knew,
And guide us to a path that's new.

So let us embrace the pain we feel,
And let it show us what's truly real,
For in our struggles we can find,
A purpose that is truly divine.

Chapter 3 – Seize The Moment

Time is a precious pearl, don't let it slip away, use it wisely and make every moment count.

In time's fleeting grasp, make every second count, for the present moment is a gift that yields a future of abundant amount.

We're all masters of our souls. Negative thoughts attract negative people and negative experiences. Positive vibrations create positive experiences. You choose your own destiny.

Did you know that everyone gets the same amount of time? That's right. Even the person sleeping on a park bench has the same amount of time as the most productive person in the world. It's how you use your time that makes all the difference and your paradigm controls that.

In the fleeting moments of life, every second counts, for the present moment is a gift that yields a future of abundant amount. Those who have embraced a paradigm shift and used their time wisely have proven this time and time again.

In the book, *The Power of Now: A Guide to Spiritual Enlightenment*, discussed in the last chapter, Eckhart Tolle emphasises the importance of having a paradigm shift and seizing the present moment as a key aspect of spiritual awakening and living a fulfilling life.

Tolle explains that most individuals spend their lives either dwelling on the past or projecting into the future, rarely fully engaging with the present moment. He argues that the present moment is the only reality and that true joy and fulfilment can only be found by fully embracing it.

According to Tolle, the mind's constant chatter and preoccupation with past and future prevent individuals from fully experiencing the present. He encourages people to become aware of this tendency and to actively choose to shift their focus to the now. By doing so, they can tap into a deeper sense of aliveness and connectedness with the present moment.

By seizing the moment and living in the present, individuals can break free from the constraints of the egotistic mind, release the burden of past regrets and future worries and connect with the deeper essence of their being. It is through this connection that true spiritual enlightenment and a more meaningful existence can be realised.

An example is Dwayne "The Rock" Johnson, who transitioned from being a professional wrestler to a Hollywood superstar. Despite starting his acting career in his mid-30s, he used his time wisely and worked tirelessly to become one of the most sought-after actors today. His work ethic and commitment to his craft are a testament to the power of a paradigm shift.

The Rock's story teaches us the importance of grabbing opportunities and taking risks now, without worrying about the past or the future. When he was offered the lead role in the movie "The Scorpion King," he took a chance and grabbed the opportunity immediately, despite it being a departure from his wrestling career. This decision led to his breakthrough in the acting world and opened doors for many more opportunities.

Furthermore, The Rock's journey proves that it is never too late to pursue your dreams and achieve success if you have the right mindset and if you can shift your paradigm. Despite facing initial rejection and setbacks in his acting career, he persevered and continued to work on his craft. His journey is a reminder that success is not just about talent or luck, but also about seizing the moment and making the most of your time. Success is also about opening yourself up to the possibility of changing the way you view the world. When things don't go as expected, trust the reroute.

At the age of 19, Adele, a British singer and songwriter, achieved a breakthrough with her debut album "19," which garnered multiple awards. She persisted in honing her craft and taking creative risks, resulting in the resounding success of her subsequent albums "21" and "25." Adele's shift in mindset towards self-belief and dedication paved the way for a thriving career in the music industry.

Adele never allowed naysayers to discourage her, as she was resolute in her conviction that validation comes from within. She believed that one need not rely on external validation to pursue their aspirations and desires. Our thoughts and emotions are a reflection of what is in the process of coming into existence and visualising our goals can materialise them into reality. If we can visualise it in our minds, we can achieve it in the physical realm.

Adele's story is testament to the power of seizing the moment and making the most of one's time. It proves that with hard work and determination, anyone can achieve their dreams. The story serves as a reminder to us all to believe in ourselves and to never give up on our aspirations. We are unlimited beings and we can always do more. American author, philosopher and mythologist, Joseph Campbell, said, "Follow your bliss and the universe will open doors for you where there were only walls". This quote has become a popular mantra for those seeking to live a more fulfilling and purposeful life. Campbell believed that when we shift our paradigm, pursue our passions and do what we love, the universe will conspire to help us achieve our goals, even in the face of seemingly insurmountable obstacles.

Serena Williams, one of the greatest tennis players of all time, is another example of someone who seized the moment, persevered and achieved massive success. Despite facing challenges and setbacks, including discrimination because of her skin colour, Serena has always maintained a positive attitude and worked tirelessly to improve her game. Her paradigm shift towards perseverance and a growth mindset has made her a role model for aspiring athletes worldwide.

Serena is a testament to the power of using time to hone one's craft. She has dedicated countless hours to her sport, consistently pushing herself to be the best she can be. Her hard work and determination have paid off as she won a record-breaking 23 Grand Slam singles titles, including seven victories at Wimbledon.

Serena's journey to success was not without its challenges. Growing up in Compton, California, she faced discrimination and adversity, but she refused to let those obstacles hold her back. Instead, she used her experiences to fuel her drive and passion for tennis. Through years of hard work and dedication, she has become one of the most dominant players in the history of the sport.

Serena's example reminds us that success is not handed to us on a silver platter; rather, it is the result of a relentless pursuit of excellence and a shift in one's paradigm. By taking advantage of the present moment and maximising our time, we can also accomplish greatness in various areas of our lives, including sports, music, writing, healthcare, or any other profession. We must embrace the present moment as a gift and use it wisely, knowing that every second counts in the pursuit of our dreams.

Bob Proctor, a renowned motivational speaker, believes that many people are stuck in a paradigm that limits their potential and this paradigm pushes them to inefficient use of their time. They fail to break free from old patterns and unproductive habits. Proctor says, "the difference between successful people and unsuccessful people is that successful people take action in the time that they have".

Tony Robbins, another motivational speaker, says that people waste time when they lack clarity and direction and that by setting clear goals and taking consistent action towards them, individuals can make breakthroughs and achieve success. It is important to recognise that time is a finite resource and that every moment counts. By embracing a sense of urgency and taking action towards their goals, individuals can maximise their potential and make breakthroughs.

These individuals are proof that a paradigm shift can have a profound impact on our lives. By using our time wisely and embracing change, we can achieve greatness in any field we choose. The present moment is a gift and it's up to us to seize it and make the most of it. Remember, every second counts in the pursuit of our dreams. By embracing a paradigm shift and focusing on our goals, we can make the most of our time and live a fulfilling life.

Bonus poem

Seize the moment, don't let it slip away,
For time is a precious gift, it won't delay.
The past is gone, the future is unknown,
But the present moment is yours alone.

Embrace each moment with open arms,
For life is fleeting, it has its charms.
The laughter, the tears, the joy and the sorrow,
All are part of life's journey, today and tomorrow.

Seize the moment, with all your might,
For it's the only moment you have in sight.
Live it, love it, make it your own,
For the present moment will soon be gone.

Chapter 4 – Confront Your Fears

Strength doesn't come from what you can do. It comes from overcoming the things you once thought you couldn't.

Celebrated motivational speaker Les Brown once said, "You can either live your dreams or live your fears." It's a statement that rings true for many people. Unfortunately, most individuals aren't living their dreams but rather their fears. Fear is an emotion that we all experience and it can be a significant obstacle that hinders us from realising our true potential.

So, I have a question for you. What are your fears? What are you afraid of? We all have something that's blocking us, that's holding us back. As we examine our lives, we come to understand that fear is the primary reason why most people don't achieve their goals or pursue their passions. Fear is often referred to as false evidence or expectations appearing real.

I'm reminded of a story told by the same Les Brown about a man who had a new neighbour with a bulldog. Every day when he came home, the bulldog would chase him about half a block. The man grew tired of this and decided to confront the bulldog. When the bulldog came running, he picked up a rock to throw at it. To his surprise, the bulldog had no teeth and it wasn't chasing him. The bulldog was enjoying the daily run with him. He had been running scared for no reason all this time. The fear was appearing real.

This is a perfect example of how we can scare ourselves to death with false expectations appearing real. Fear can be paralysing and it can prevent us from achieving our goals. It's essential to confront our fears and understand that most of the time, they're not as big as we make them out to be. Our faith is tested many times by fear before we are crowned to victory.

We should strive to live our dreams and not our fears. We mustn't let fear hold us back from pursuing our passions and living fulfilling lives. Instead, we should confront our fears, examine them closely and understand that most of the time, they're just false expectations appearing real. So, don't let your fears control you. Live life boldly and fearlessly.

There are some people who get a kick out of scaring themselves to death. An example can be found in Stephen King's novel "IT". It is a horror story that follows a group of childhood friends, known as the "Losers' Club," as they confront an ancient evil that has been terrorising their town of Derry, Maine for centuries. The entity, which takes on the form of a clown named Pennywise, preys on the fears of its victims and has the ability to shape-shift into whatever form is most terrifying to the person it is targeting.

The story is told through both the perspectives of the characters as children and as adults, as they reunite after 27 years to once again face the entity and put an end to its reign of terror. Along the way, they must confront their deepest fears and traumas and come to terms with the fact that they may not be able to defeat the entity alone.

Eddie Kaspbrak is a hypochondriac who is constantly afraid of getting sick or injured. This fear is exploited by the entity, which takes on the form of a leper and tells Eddie that he is contaminated and needs to be cleansed. Another character in the book, Beverly, is afraid of her abusive father, who she believes is sexually attracted to her. The entity takes on the form of her father and tries to lure her into its clutches. Henry Bowers is a bully who is afraid of losing his power and being seen as weak. The entity takes advantage of this fear and manipulates him into becoming its servant. Lastly, Mike Hanlon is the only black member of the group and he is afraid of the racism and violence that he sees in his community. The entity takes on the form of a giant bird and attacks him, playing on his fear of being persecuted.

The last frightening quote from "IT" is where the protagonist Bill Denbrough confronts the shape-shifting monster and says, "He thrusts his fists against the posts and still insists he sees the ghosts." Denbrough was repeatedly trying to convince himself that he was seeing ghosts, even though there was no evidence to support this belief. He had the stubbornness or determination to believe in something that was not rational or logical.

Overall, the novel explores the idea that fear is a powerful force that can be exploited by those who seek to do harm. It also suggests that facing one's fears can be a way to overcome even the most terrifying challenges. It's a poignant reminder that sometimes we're our own worst enemies and the things that scare us the most are the things we create in our own minds. But it doesn't have to be that way. We can learn to face our fears head-on and overcome them, just like the guy in the story with the bulldog. All it takes is a little bit of courage and the willingness to take a risk.

I vividly remember the horror movie "The Exorcist" that I watched when I was much younger. The experience was so terrifying that it was etched in my memory for many years. I was so scared that when I returned home from the cinema, I immediately went straight to bed. At that moment, I was completely out of my wits.

However, there are people who face their fears head-on. For instance, my late friend George had no fear whatsoever. He could speak in public, talk to strangers and confront anyone. He made a lot of money because of his power to convince anyone to buy the music records that he was selling at the time. I greatly admired him for his courage. Growing up, I aspired to be as brave as him. Yet, fear sometimes held me back from pursuing my dreams. It prevented me from doing the things I loved until I shifted my mindset, my paradigm.

If fear has been preventing you from living your best life, it's time to take action. Abraham Maslow once said that life is all about growth. You can either remain in your comfort zone, where you won't experience any growth, or take a step forward and face your fears head-on.

It's essential to acknowledge that fear is a natural emotion that everyone experiences at some point in their life. Therefore, don't be too hard on yourself if you feel afraid. Embrace your fears and use them as a motivator to propel yourself forward. By doing so, you'll realise that the more you resist your fears, the more they persist.

However, it's also important to acknowledge that some fears are legitimate and should be taken seriously. For instance, the fear of bodily harm is genuine and you should always proceed with caution in such situations. Facing your fears is the first step towards achieving your goals and living your best life. Don't let fear hold you back. Instead, embrace it, acknowledge it and use it as a motivator to propel yourself forward.

By challenging fear and seeking out the truth, we can begin to break free from the limitations that it imposes on us.

Living a life free from fear doesn't mean that we'll never experience discomfort or uncertainty. It simply means that we won't let those things hold us back from pursuing our dreams and living up to our full potential. On the other side of fear lies a world of endless possibilities.

Bonus poem

Confront your fears, don't let them hold you back,
Take a deep breath, don't let courage slack.
It's natural to be scared, but don't let it control,
Your life, your dreams, your ultimate goal.

Step by step, face your fears with pride,
Don't let them run, don't let them hide.
The power is yours, you have the strength within,
Confront your fears, let the victory begin.

With every step, you gain more ground,
Your confidence grows, your fears unbound.
Confront your fears and watch them fade,
And in their place, a new life is made.

Chapter 5 – Discipline Your Thinking

By disciplining our thoughts, we can direct our focus towards positive and productive thinking, which in turn can lead to the manifestation of our goals and dreams.

Discipline is choosing between what you want now and what you want most. - Abraham Lincoln

The pain of discipline is far less than the pain of regret. - Sarah Bombell

As a writer who has worked in many situations where speaking is required, I have learned the importance of monitoring my inner dialogue and maintaining discipline in my thoughts and imagination. Failure to do so can result in our minds taking us on a wild ride, failing to shift our mindset.

I recall a moment when I was in a meeting and heard the presenters across from me discussing their many accomplishments. I began doubting myself and became fearful that I could not compete with them. I even considered not going through with my presentation.

However, I knew that I needed to talk to myself and reframe my thinking. So, I excused myself and went to the bathroom to have a conversation with myself. I reminded myself that I had two children to feed, a sick mother to care for and a home to provide for. I had nothing to lose and everything to gain by going through with my presentation. I told myself that I would not let these people intimidate me and I would not back down until I presented a great speech.

Talking to oneself may seem like an odd exercise, but it can be a powerful tool in self-motivation. We must be intentional in our self-talk and avoid casual, negative chatter. By positively affirming ourselves and answering our doubts, we can build ourselves up and increase our energy levels. Others will sense this confidence and it will radiate through our actions and words.

As we journey through life, it is important to realise that self-doubt can be sensed by others. People can pick up on the self-doubt we radiate, which is why it is crucial to stand up for ourselves.

A story is told of a little boy on a bus who was being bullied by some bigger boys. They were thumping him on the head and he wanted to move away from them. However, every time he stood up to leave, they pushed him back down. But he persevered and kept standing up, even when they pushed him down again.

Eventually, they held him down and he said, "You might hold me down, but I'm standing up inside myself."

We all have something within us that we are capable of doing. It is not optional to sit on what we have been given. Each of us has something to offer to the world that only we can do, perform, or initiate. If we do not fill our lives with our life's work or mission, there will be gaps in our lives. When we are not living out our true identity, we begin to fill those gaps with garbage such as worry and self-destructive behaviour. If you know that you are not doing what you can do because you have allowed yourself to be held captive by your fears, it is time to take action.

If you do not have a true appreciation and acceptance of who you are and allow yourself to be immobilised by fear, you begin to abuse yourself. You sabotage your life, your dreams and work against yourself unconsciously, becoming your worst enemy.

But you can overcome this by acknowledging your true identity and the power and capacity within you to bring about change. Your hunger for your dreams and your gifts will begin to push you past your fear. Your hunger to achieve your dreams will give you a special drive as you work on yourself.

A man who was doing a special study of a tribe in Africa had difficulty developing a relationship with the tribesmen due to his fear that they would take his head. After working there for a long time with no progress, he realised that he needed to overcome his fear.

He asked himself, "What is it that you came here to do? What is your life's work?"

He decided that he was going to do it, come what may and he stopped being afraid.

The next day, he talked to and interviewed many members of the tribe and they responded positively to him.

Most of the fears we have are blown out of proportion by our imagination. We give them more power than they deserve and we allow them to govern our lives and determine how far we can stretch towards our dreams and potential. When life can no longer threaten us with death, what else is there?

By being our own motivators, we can overcome any obstacle that comes our way. We can push past our doubts and fears and achieve greatness. But it all starts with the conversations we have with ourselves.

I understand that talking to oneself may not come naturally to everyone. However, it is a skill that can be developed with practice. One way to start is by setting aside a few minutes each day to affirm ourselves positively. It may seem awkward at first, but over time, it will become second nature.

Remember, the mind is a powerful tool and we must learn to use it to our advantage. By taking control of our thoughts and imagination, we can create a positive and successful life for ourselves. So let's start talking to ourselves and building ourselves up. The results will amaze us.

When faced with self-doubt, it can be tempting to listen to our inner critic and give up on our goals. However, sometimes the best thing we can do is talk to ourselves and become our own cheerleaders.

It's important to remember that our thoughts and beliefs have a powerful impact on our actions and outcomes. If we let negative self-talk control us, we may miss out on opportunities and limit our potential. By talking to ourselves in a positive and encouraging way, we can build up our confidence and overcome obstacles.

Of course, talking to oneself isn't a substitute for seeking help or advice from others when we need it. However, by becoming our own motivators, we can develop a greater sense of self-reliance and inner strength. We can cultivate a mindset of positivity and resilience, even when things get tough and we can begin to change our paradigm.

Bonus poem

Discipline your thinking, let your imagination fly,
Channel your thoughts, to the stars in the sky.
For your mind is a garden, where ideas take root,
So plant the right seeds and they'll bear wondrous fruit.

Focus on the positive, the possible, the good,
Train your brain to see, what others never could.
Let your imagination soar, with no limits or bounds,
And your thoughts will be clear, like sweet, harmonious
sounds.

With discipline and practice, your mind will be free,
To explore new horizons, that others never see.
So cultivate your thoughts, with purpose and care,
And your imagination will lead you, anywhere.

Discipline your thinking, to achieve your wildest dreams,
And your imagination will light the path, like sunbeams.

Chapter 6 – Nurture Your Hunger for Success

When you're hungry for success, don't let anyone feed you crap about slowing down. - Marie Forleo

A lion runs the fastest when he is hunger - Salman Khan

Many of us have come to realise that if we want to achieve something significant in life, change our behaviour, or overcome negative habits, it is not an easy task. Despite the claims of some people who make it seem effortless, living your dream and making changes in your life can be challenging and demanding.

I once heard a song by a guy named Dimples called "If it ain't one thing, it's another." This sentiment rings true because in life, there is always something going on. You will never have a moment free of problems and as the saying goes, "You're either in a problem, just left a problem, or heading towards one." It is a reality that we must accept. But more importantly, it is important to realise that our hunger for success comes from the depths of our soul. If there's no enemy within, the enemy outside can do us no harm.

You have to change how you see yourself to achieve success.

So, how can we nurture the hunger and drive to succeed?

What are the qualities of people who are hungry for success and what does it take to achieve what we want?

Firstly, we must work on ourselves. It is vital to engage in an ongoing process of self-development and spend more time investing in ourselves. We must read books, attend courses and seminars and prioritise our growth and have faith that we will succeed. But this faith will always be tested. Faith not tested cannot be trusted.

In his book *The University of Success*, Og Mandino wrote a line that gave me chills: "Many of us never realise our greatness because we become sidetracked by secondary activity, by challenges that test our faith". This statement by Og Mandino is a powerful reminder of the importance of staying focused on our goals and priorities. It's easy to get caught up in secondary activities, such as social media, television, or other distractions that can take us away from our true purpose in life.

The pursuit of greatness requires a dedication to the primary activities that will lead us to success. We must be willing to invest our time, energy and resources into the activities that will help us achieve our goals, rather than allowing ourselves to be sidetracked by things that won't ultimately matter.

Mandino's words highlight the fact that many people fail to realise their full potential because they lose sight of what is truly important. It's all too common to get caught up in the mundane tasks of daily life and forget about the bigger picture. By focusing on what truly matters, we can avoid becoming sidetracked by secondary activities and instead achieve the greatness we are capable of.

I remember a time when I was trying to sell Yellow Pages books on the phone when I came to the UK in the early 1990s. At first, I took it personally when people said no. But eventually, I began to view it as a game. I knew that there was someone out there who would say yes and I was determined to keep calling those landline phones until I found that person. And sure enough, someone eventually said yes and then there were 10 of them, 20, 30 and more.

Years later I was working as a software coder after graduating from university. I was terrible and I my six month contract was not renewed. At the time, I felt like my life was out of control. But eventually, I realised that I had the power to take control of my destiny. I started working harder than ever before and I began to see results.

It's easy to be negative or to give in to mediocrity. But if we want to be successful, we must develop the habit of giving more than what is expected of us. We must set high standards for ourselves and strive to be the best we can be, even in difficult circumstances. Thomas Eddison failed 1,400 times before he invented the light bulb. Thank God he failed that many times and still remained on course.

So wherever you are and whatever you are doing, give it your all. Develop the habit of going above and beyond and you will leave a trail for others to follow. And if you need inspiration or motivation, just remember the words of Churchill – "Courage is going from failure to failure without losing enthusiasm."

American theatre and film producer, known for his successful productions such as "Around the World in 80 Days" and "Oklahoma", Michael Todd, says we must make time for ourselves because our lives are our own productions. We are the stars, directors and scriptwriters and we determine whether our lives are a smash hit or a flop. He believed that it was important to make time for ourselves because our lives are our own productions.

We have the power to shape our own destiny and determine whether our lives will be a success or failure. Just like in a theatre or film production, we must take ownership of our roles and responsibilities. This means that we must take the time to nurture ourselves and our goals and make conscious choices that align with our values and aspirations. We must not let external circumstances or other people dictate the direction of our lives. Instead, we must take charge and create the life we want.

We must talk to ourselves, work on empowering ourselves and overcome negative self-talk. Our inner dialogue is constantly ongoing and even when we do not want it to, it can be detrimental to our success. We must learn to stand up to ourselves and say, "Shut up!" At that point, we can replace negative self-talk with positive thoughts that shift our paradigm.

It's not enough to just work on yourself, though. In addition to personal development, hungry people also have a clear vision of what they want and the determination to go after it. They often have a deep desire to contribute to something greater than them, whether it's their community, a cause they believe in, or a vision for a better future.

They are willing to face challenges, setbacks and failures along the way and use them as opportunities to learn and grow. It means refusing to give up or settle for less than what you truly want. So if you want to live a life of purpose and fulfilment, if you want to achieve your goals and make a difference in the world, cultivate that hunger within yourself. Work on yourself, create a clear vision and embrace a mindset of perseverance and resilience. And remember, it's never too late to start. As long as you're alive, you have the opportunity to make your dreams a reality.

Winston Churchill once said that courage is the ability to persevere through failure without losing enthusiasm. It takes a great deal of courage to face our fears and continue to push ourselves towards our goals. But when we do, something remarkable happens; we are able to transcend ourselves and reach new heights.

Bonus poem

Nurture your hunger, let it grow and thrive,
For the taste of success, you must constantly strive.
Let your passion ignite like a burning flame,
And let your drive push you beyond any shame.

Feed your ambition with a relentless desire,
And let your spirit soar higher and higher.
Let every obstacle fuel your hunger for more,
And every setback make you stronger than before.

Nurture your hunger, let it consume your being,
For only then can you achieve what you are seeing.
Believe in yourself and your potential to excel,
And with hard work and dedication, you shall prevail.

Chapter 7 – The Power of Incremental Progress

Every action you take is a vote for the type of person you wish to become. No single instance will transform your beliefs, but as the votes build up, so does the evidence of your new identity. - James Clear, 'Atomic Habits'

The power of incremental progress is the antidote to overwhelm and doubt, turning big dreams into manageable goals.

Step by step, we can climb the mountain of our aspirations, guided by the power of incremental progress.

Life is precious and time is a valuable commodity that we can never recover. If we waste our time, we risk not fulfilling our potential, which can cause psychological damage and reflect negatively on our personalities. We must set high standards for ourselves and develop a sense of urgency to make the most of the time we have. It is important to develop a sense of urgency in life and how we can nurture this quality within ourselves.

If you have something you want to accomplish, don't put it off until it's too late. Instead, do just a little bit of it at a time. Robert Schuller said, "By the yard, it's hard, but inch-by-inch anything is essential." The above quote from James Clear's book, Atomic Habits, speaks to the power of incremental progress in creating lasting change.

By making small, consistent actions towards our desired identity or goals, we can shift our paradigm by building up evidence of our new identity over time. In other words, every time we make a positive choice, we are casting a vote for the type of person we want to be. With each vote, we strengthen our belief in our new identity and move closer to achieving it.

Bobby Kerr, an Irish entrepreneur and former Dragon on Dragons' Den, has spoken about the importance of incremental progress and the dangers of failing to use atomic habits to shift your paradigm and achieve success.

Kerr has emphasised that success is not a one-time event, but rather the result of consistent effort and small, incremental improvements over time. He believes that people often fail to achieve their goals because they focus too much on the end result and not enough on the daily habits and routines that will get them there.

According to Kerr, using atomic habits, or small, consistent actions that compound over time, is key to achieving long-term success. By breaking down larger goals into smaller, more manageable tasks and consistently working towards them, individuals can build momentum and make progress towards their desired outcome. On the other hand, failing to use atomic habits can lead to stagnation or even regression. Without consistent effort and a focus on incremental progress, it is easy to fall into old habits and lose sight of our goals.

Bonus poem

The power of incremental progress,
May seem like a slow process,
But it's the small steps that pave the way,
To achieve your goals day by day.

Each step may seem insignificant,
But over time they become magnificent,
Like drops of water forming a stream,
Leading you to where you dream.

Celebrate each step, no matter how small,
For they add up and make you stand tall,
With perseverance and patience in your heart,
You'll see how incremental progress sets you apart.

Chapter 8 – Harness Your Creative Energy

Your brain is the ultimate supercomputer processing 20,901 million pieces of information every second. You're only conscious of 40 of those only. The rest is in your subconscious.

Thought is energy.

Mind is the ultimate weaver. - James Allen

In the depths of our minds, lies a wellspring of creative energy, waiting to be harnessed and unleashed. When we tap into this source of inspiration, we can create revolutionary ideas that challenge existing paradigms and reshape our world. It is a truism that the ultimate resource is resourcefulness as it shifts our paradigm and allows us to achieve beyond our expectations.

In order to achieve something you've never achieved before, you have to become someone you've never been before. You have to become a totally different human being, not just a simple version of yourself. You have to dream big dreams and use your creative energy to achieve those dreams. This is very possible because every human is hardwired to do something special with their life. You cannot aim and hit a target that you can't see; otherwise you will just be fumbling in the dark.

Take the example of Marie Curie, whose work in radioactivity revolutionised our understanding of physics and medicine. Curie was a pioneering scientist who used her creativity and intellectual curiosity to explore the mysteries of the atomic world. Through her research, she uncovered groundbreaking insights into the fundamental building blocks of matter, which revolutionised our understanding of physics and medicine.

Her work on radioactivity challenged the existing paradigm in the field of physics, which assumed that atoms were indivisible and unchanging. Her discoveries showed that atoms were actually composed of smaller subatomic particles that were constantly in motion, emitting energy and radiation. In this way, Curie's work transformed our understanding of the physical world and opened up new avenues for research and innovation in fields such as nuclear energy and medicine. By harnessing her creative energy and pursuing her intellectual curiosity, Curie was able to make significant contributions to the scientific community and the world as a whole. This would not have happened without her paradigm shift and her creative energy.

Similarly, Steve Jobs used his creative energy to transform the technology industry, with the creation of the iPhone and other revolutionary products. He challenged the prevailing paradigm that technology was solely the domain of experts and geeks, making it accessible and user-friendly for the masses.

But harnessing creative energy is not just the domain of scientists and entrepreneurs. It can be found in every aspect of life, from the arts to social justice movements.
The feminist movement, for example, harnessed the creative energy of women across the world, challenging traditional gender roles and norms. From the suffragette movement to the #MeToo movement, women have used their creativity to demand equal rights and representation.

Even in our personal lives, we can harness our creative energy to spark paradigm shifts. By breaking out of our comfort zones and exploring new ways of thinking and being, we can transform ourselves and our relationships. When we harness our creative energy, we tap into a force that can move mountains and change the course of history. Ultimately, any activity that challenges our assumptions and encourages us to think outside of our comfort zone can help us harness creative energy to shift our paradigm.

To grow and learn in life, it's important to be open-minded and curious. This means being willing to consider new ideas and ways of looking at things. It also means breaking out of our usual ways of thinking and doing things and not being controlled by our emotions from the past. Don't try and fix old broken ideas, try and create something new, using your creative energy. Create a new reality and don't be a victim to your environment.

How uncomfortable do you have to be before you make up your mind to use your creative energy and change your paradigm?

I created a simple strategy and I made a paradigm shift. I overcome myself every morning and the rest of the day is great. I connect to the energy of the future; not the past. I do not use my past to reaffirm my identity. I use my creativity to construct my future.

If you think about it, all problems are memories of the past; of certain people, objects and certain times and places. The moment you abandon your creativity and focus on your problems, you're stuck. You're thinking in the past and there is no creativity in the past, only in the future. To create new things, you have to rebrand the circulatory in your brain. This is very important because humans are conditioned to lie to themselves. They have an illusion of success and are limited by weakness of attention and poverty of imagination. To change your future, you have to be able to use your creative energy to change your paradigm.

Robert Heinlein says, "In absence of clearly defined goals, we become strangely loyal to performing daily trivia until we ultimately become enslaved by it." This statement is clear on what kills our creativity and stops us from shifting our paradigm. People tend to get stuck in a routine of mundane tasks and activities. They become so accustomed to this routine that they no longer question it and they may even become trapped or enslaved by it, losing sight of their power of creativity.

Bonus poem

Let your mind wander and roam,
For creativity to find a home.
With each idea, let it bloom and grow,
And watch your imagination overflow.

Harness that energy, let it flow,
Watch it take flight, watch it glow.
See the world in a brand new light,
Let your creativity take flight.

With every stroke of the pen or brush,
See your ideas turn into a rush.
Nurture that spark, let it ignite,
And watch your creativity take flight.

Chapter 9 – Unleash Creativity with Your Subconscious Mind

The subconscious mind is a supercomputer, capable of processing information at a speed that is almost unimaginable. When you tap into its power, there is nothing you cannot achieve.. - Brian Tracy

The subconscious mind is the source of all creativity and inspiration. It is where our true genius lies, waiting to be unlocked. - Deepak Chopra

The subconscious mind is like a garden. Whatever you plant in it will grow and flourish. So be mindful of your thoughts, for they shape your reality. - Itayi Garande.

In the last chapter we discussed the importance of harnessing your creative energy to make extraordinary achievements. But how do we harness that creative energy? Writers have suggested several ways to do so, including setting clear goals and objectives that you want to achieve. This will help focus your creative energy on specific outcomes. Others have suggested engaging in activities that stimulate your creativity, such as brainstorming, mindmapping, or other creative exercises. Still others have called for keeping an open mind and being receptive to new ideas and perspectives. This will help you to approach problems and challenges from different angles and find innovative solutions.

However, real changes, real paradigm shifts occur when you can master your subconscious mind by positive affirmations, destroying negative feelings, jealousy, envy and practising mindfulness. These help you live in the present, tapping into your subconscious mind where all the "gold" is located. The conscious mind is too distracted and distracting.

Our subconscious mind has a way of picking up on things that our conscious mind might miss. When we're working on a creative project, our subconscious mind can help us tap into our intuition and make connections that we might not have made otherwise. For example, famous inventor Nikola Tesla said that many of his best ideas came to him in flashes of intuition that he couldn't explain.

We all experience creative blocks from time to time. When this happens, it can be helpful to take a break and let our subconscious mind take over for a while. By stepping away from the problem and giving our subconscious time to work on it, we may find that new solutions or ideas emerge without conscious effort. This is why many people report having breakthrough ideas while taking a shower, going for a walk, or engaging in some other activity that allows their mind to wander.

Dreams can be a rich source of creative inspiration. While we sleep, our subconscious mind is free to roam and make connections that we might not make when we're awake. Many famous works of art, literature and music have been inspired by dreams.

Rhonda Byrne, an Australian television writer and producer, best known for her book "The Secret" and subsequent documentary film of the same name, says the subconscious mind is 'perfectly divine' meaning that it is capable of achieving great things and has the power to bring positive changes to our lives. She suggests that we train our subconscious mind through positive affirmations and visualisation techniques. By doing so, we can unlock our full potential and achieve our goals.

Paul McCartney came up with the melody for the song "Yesterday." McCartney has said that he woke up one morning with the melody in his head and initially assumed that it must have been a song he had heard before. But after playing it for various people and realising that no one recognised it, he realised that it was an original creation that had come to him in a dream or during a state of half-sleep.

The melody had been generated by his subconscious mind and he was able to bring it into consciousness and turn it into one of the most famous and beloved songs of all time.

Another example is the story of how J.K. Rowling came up with the idea for the Harry Potter series. Rowling has said that the idea came to her on a train journey and that the character and world of Harry Potter seemed to arrive fully formed in her mind. She later realised that the idea had been simmering in her subconscious for some time and that it was a product of her deepest desires and fears. By tapping into her subconscious mind and trusting her intuition, Rowling was able to create a hugely successful and beloved series of books that have captured the imaginations of millions of people around the world.

The idea is that everything is possible when we tap into our subconscious mind and believe that it creates everything. This is because it always acts in the present, not the past. If you say to yourself, "I am successful," the subconscious mind believes you and manifests your life to be in tune with that affirmation. It doesn't fight your affirmation.

Similarly, if you say, "I am poor and ineffective," the subconscious believes you and manifests your poverty and ineffectiveness. It is not the duty of the subconscious mind to fight your affirmations. It acts in the present. If you say, "A new car is coming," it will always be coming in the "eyes" of the subconscious, so you have to say something like, "Thanks for my new car." You have to imagine it here already. Otherwise it will always be a desire that is in the future, not present. The subconscious will record it as having been achieved in the future and finished.

The subconscious mind can support creativity by generating new ideas, associations and connections that the conscious mind might not be able to make. It can also help us access our intuition and inner wisdom, which can be important sources of creative inspiration.

The subconscious doesn't know that you are imagining things. It is always in the present. It is your pot of gold, your Midas touch, your superpower, your holy grail. You can use it to shift your paradigm and harness your creativity. It is the gateway to the universe and can bring about profound changes in one's life. By harnessing the power of the subconscious mind, we can transform our thoughts, beliefs and actions to achieve our goals and live our best lives.

Bonus poem

Unlock the doors of your mind,
And let your creativity unwind.
With your subconscious at play,
New ideas will come your way.

It's a realm beyond our control,
Where inspiration takes its toll.
Let your thoughts roam free and wild,
And let your imagination be riled.

For in the depths of your mind,
Lies the creativity you'll find.

So embrace the power within,
And let your subconscious win.

Unleash your creativity with pride,
And let it be your ultimate guide.
For with your subconscious in tow,
Limitations you'll never know.

Chapter 10 – Ignite Purpose with Passion

Don't ask yourself what the world needs. Ask yourself what makes you come alive and then go do that. Because what the world needs is people who have come alive. - Howard Thurman

We're born into genius, but many of us get resigned in apathy and mediocrity.

We may not be perfect people and our situations may not be perfect either, but we still have a purpose and we are significant. We have been blessed with a rich body of emotions that distinguishes us from plants and bushes. We have feelings and when we use them properly, they are very effective in motivating us towards our destiny. Passion and purpose are interconnected and it is essential to understand this relationship.

Unfortunately, we live in a fast-paced world and we are often too busy to connect with our inner sense of passion. However, it is our passion that empowers us to accomplish what we were created to do. Passion is what propels us forward and helps us to function at a higher dimension with authority and conviction. It is that higher dimension that allows us to make a paradigm shift. It also helps us to overcome the obstacles that come with fulfilling our purpose.

Even if you haven't yet identified your purpose, it is important to at least get in the territory of the thing you hope to accomplish. Through passion, you will be able to ignite things you never thought possible. It's not uncommon to feel like you don't have any passion at times, but the key is to get exposed and get involved in new experiences. This way, you will be able to see that there are more options available to you than what your current situation presents.

Life comes with its fair share of challenges and pains and it is essential to acknowledge them. However, it is important to note that these challenges are not distractions from our purpose.

In fact, the pain we experience helps to fuel the burning desire to achieve our purpose. Extraordinary feats often come with extraordinary challenges and it is our passion that gives us the power we need to overcome them.

We are like arrows that need to be directed towards the things we want them to hit. However, we don't push an arrow; we pull it away from the target. Yet, it is the digression that causes the progression and sometimes the challenges we face in life are just pulling us back so that we can be released towards our purpose.

So, there is no need to grieve over what we didn't get or how we were treated in the past. Instead, we can use these experiences to push us towards fulfilling our purpose.

At any age, we can ignite our purpose by finding our passion. That is the good news.
You don't have to grieve over what you didn't get and what didn't happen and how you were treated and who didn't raise you. None of that matters because now you're in the game and the pain that you experienced is simply the arrow being pulled back so that you can go forward with more power and accuracy.

Thuli Madonsela, a South African human rights lawyer and former Public Protector, found her purpose by igniting her passion and made a big paradigm shift. Despite experiencing discrimination and marginalisation during apartheid, Madonsela pursued her passion for law and justice, eventually becoming the first woman to hold the position of Public Protector in South Africa.

Through her work, Madonsela fought against corruption and advocated for transparency and accountability in government, earning widespread respect and admiration both in South Africa and internationally.

Despite facing numerous obstacles and challenges throughout her career, Madonsela persevered and made a significant impact in promoting justice and equality for all. Her story is a testament to the power of finding one's passion and purpose and the ability to overcome adversity in pursuit of one's dreams.

Another example of a paradigm shift ignited by adversity is that of Chris Kirubi, a Kenyan businessman and entrepreneur who passed away in 2021. Kirubi started his career in sales and marketing, but eventually found his passion in entrepreneurship.

He founded several successful companies, including Capital FM, one of Kenya's leading radio stations and Haco Industries, a consumer goods manufacturer. Kirubi's success was not without its challenges. He faced financial difficulties and even battled cancer. However, he persevered through these obstacles and continued to pursue his passion for entrepreneurship. He also used his success to give back to his community, supporting education and mentorship programs for young people in Kenya.

Kirubi's story is a testament to the power of finding and following your passion, regardless of your age or background. With hard work and determination, anyone can achieve their goals and make a positive impact on the world.

Remember, passion and purpose are interconnected. Your passion will empower you to fulfill your purpose and the pain you've experienced will give you the conviction to pursue it.

Emotions are a rich part of our human experience and they can be very effective in motivating us towards our destiny. However, we live in a busy world that often makes it difficult to stay connected to our inner sense of passion.

The good news is that you don't have to be perfect and you don't have to have a perfect situation to ignite your purpose. You simply need to find your passion and get involved. Passion will give you the thrust you need to accomplish the things you were created to do, even when faced with obstacles.

So, if you're feeling disconnected from your passion, take some time to expose yourself to new experiences, get involved and connect with others. At any age, you can still ignite your purpose by finding your passion and make that important paradigm shift.

We may not be perfect and we may face challenges in life, but we are still significant and capable of accomplishing extraordinary things. By finding our passion and staying connected to our emotions, we can empower ourselves to fulfill our purpose and pursue our dreams with conviction and determination.

Bonus poem

Passion is the flame that fuels our soul,
That ignites our purpose, makes us whole.
It drives us to seek and never give in,

To rise above, to fight and to win.

It's the fire in our belly, the spark in our eye,
The driving force that makes us fly.
It's the reason we wake up and face the day,
The fuel that makes us push past the fray.

So let your passion burn bright and true,
Let it guide and inspire all that you do.
For with it, you'll find your purpose clear,
And the strength to overcome all fear.

Chapter 11 – Embrace the Power of Possibility

To all the other dreamers out there, don't ever stop or let the world's negativity disenchant you or your spirit. If you surround yourself with love and the right people, anything is possible. - Adam Green

I live in an abundant universe where anything is possible. - NLE Choppa

A man's life is dyed in the colour of his imagination and it is what his thoughts make it. - Marcus Aurelius, Great Roman Emperor

The human mind doesn't care what you plant in it. What you plant is what it returns. - Itayi Garande

Disability is not inability. Keep pushing on. The sky is the limit. You can achieve anything you set your mind to. - Jairos Jiri, Zimbabwean philanthropist

George Bernard Shaw said that, "People are always blaming their circumstances for what they are. I don't believe in circumstances. The people who get on in this world are the people who get up and look for the circumstances they want and, if they can't find them, make them." This quote encapsulates the notion that we have the power to shape our own lives. It challenges us to step out of the victim mindset and take responsibility for our own destiny. The circumstances we face in life do not define us, nor do they limit us. Instead, they present us with opportunities to grow and shape our future.

We must become the architects of our own lives, creating the conditions we desire through hard work, determination and a willingness to take risks. We have the power to transform our reality, to shape it in accordance with our own vision and to overcome any obstacle that stands in our way. So let us not blame our circumstances for what we are, but rather, let us take charge of our lives and make the circumstances that we want. We must act as though it were impossible to fail.

In short, everything or anything is possible.

Perhaps you are working on a project and you have been hit with many obstacles, setbacks and defeats. Perhaps you are feeling discouraged and you need some motivation to get back in the game. Let's take a look at this situation from a different perspective. There are winners, losers and people who haven't discovered how to win. These individuals just need coaching, assistance, support, insight, or a new strategy to open up a new future that will give them access to their inner power.

So, let's think about something you want for yourself that is meaningful and powerful. Don't assume that you can't achieve it, but rather repeat to yourself, "It's possible."

This statement changes your belief system and makes you operate out of your imagination instead of your memory. Your imagination will allow you to see yourself achieving your goals, while your memory might tell you that it's impossible.

Most people tend to believe that things are the way they are and can't be changed. However, there are examples of individuals who have shattered these beliefs, such as Roger Bannister, who broke the four-minute barrier for running a mile. Once this was achieved, it opened up the possibility for over 20,000 people to do the same, including high school students.

In order to achieve your dreams, you must embrace your own greatness and make a meaningful contribution to the world. While it may be great to have a strong economy, favourable lending conditions, positive attitudes and a lack of opposition, the most critical element in making things happen in your life is you.

When Zimbabwean footballer, Peter Ndlovu, desired to appear on television playing for a top English football team, he was initially told that it was impossible. However, he refused to be deterred, saying to himself, "Why can't I do it?" He persisted in his quest, training hard, seeking out people who could help him, leveraging relationships and gathering the necessary skills to play at international level. He didn't take "no" for an answer and ultimately achieved his goal and was signed by and played for, Coventry City FC in the English Premier League during the 1990s.

Ndlovu was the first African player to play in the English Premier League. It was a dream come true for Ndlovu, who had always dreamed of playing in one of the top leagues in Europe.

While Ndlovu's talent was evident, playing abroad was not without its challenges. For starters, he had to adapt to a completely different culture, climate and playing style. Moreover, he had to contend with the pressure of being the first African player in the Premier League, with all the expectations that came with it.

Despite these challenges, Ndlovu persevered and quickly established himself as a key player for Coventry City. His speed, skill and goal-scoring ability quickly made him a fan favourite and he was soon regarded as one of the best strikers in the league.

However, Ndlovu's time at Coventry City was not without its setbacks. In 1992, he was involved in a serious car accident that left him with a broken leg and several other injuries. Many thought that his career was over, but Ndlovu refused to give up. He underwent months of gruelling rehabilitation and returned to the pitch stronger and more determined than ever.

In total, he scored 39 goals in 176 appearances for the club, becoming one of their all-time greats. He was also a key member of the team that won the 1997 FA Cup, the club's first major trophy in their 104-year history.

Ndlovu's legacy at Coventry City extends far beyond his on-field achievements. He was a trailblazer for African players in the Premier League, paving the way for future generations of players from the continent. Moreover, his perseverance and resilience in the face of adversity continue to inspire footballers around the world to this day.

Ndlovu's story is one of perseverance, dedication and resilience in the face of numerous setbacks and obstacles.

Don't allow the opinions of others to determine the possibilities for your dreams. It's their business, not yours. Your business is to change your paradigm and know that "It's possible." People who lack imagination live in the past and are unable to envision new possibilities. They judge according to appearances and conclude that things can't be done because they haven't seen them. But the people who make it in the future and those who are currently successful are the ones with imagination. They are the ones who write history.

To achieve your dreams, you must take personal responsibility for making them happen. Don't give up when you face opposition or experience setbacks. Seek out the help of others who can provide the energy and resources you need to move forward. Realise that obstacles and setbacks are part of the journey and that, as long as you're alive, you have a chance to achieve your dreams. Every day, remind yourself that it's not over until you win.

You must have the courage and determination to persevere, even when things get tough. If you want to succeed, you must take personal responsibility and own your vision. Whether you're working to improve your well-being, make a difference in your community, or create an economic renaissance, you must be willing to do the work to make it happen. There may be many obstacles along the way, but ultimately, success depends on you.

Somewhere on this vast planet, there is someone who has achieved what you aspire to. Their story can serve as a model for you, but it doesn't matter what colour your skin is, where you were born, or what limits your friends and family have. The only thing that truly matters is what you believe is possible for yourself. The answer must be anything. Anything is possible, but only if you truly believe it.

If you believe that anything is impossible, then that will become your reality. If you think that there are limits to what you can achieve because of excuses such as limited opportunities, where you live, or lack of funds, those limits will become your reality because you won't even attempt to do something outside of your limited mindset. Those who believe that anything is possible will try anything and attempt to achieve greatness no matter what the odds are.

Many people have gone from having nothing to achieving something, from feeling hopeless to becoming great and from having limited resources to building a legacy. If they can do it, then so can you, but only if you believe. Believing that anything is possible is one thing, but achieving something incredible is something else entirely.

Therefore, make a plan and go out there to achieve your goals. When you face setbacks or failure, keep going and learn from the experience. Everyone who has achieved greatness has experienced setbacks, but they didn't give up. Instead, they kept going and made their plan better and stronger. Remember, anything is possible if you believe in yourself.

Don't worry about the things you don't have, or what people say about you. You were born with a gift and a purpose and you have the potential to create greatness. Focus on the things that matter most to you and watch as greatness unfolds. Anything is possible if you believe.

Bonus poem

It is possible, oh yes it is,
To reach the stars, to touch the bliss.
To climb the mountains, cross the seas,

To chase the dreams and break the freeze.

It is possible, if you believe,
To overcome and to achieve.
To find your voice, to sing your song,
To rise above and to stay strong.

So take a step and then one more,
The path will lead you to the shore.
Believe in you and in your light,
And you will conquer any height.

Chapter 12 – The Perfect Time Is Now

The perfect time is now. Don't wait for the stars to align or for the perfect moment to arrive.

The future is created in the present, so make the most of it.

Remember, there is no such thing as a perfect time, only the time you have right now. Seize it and make it count.

Our thoughts and perceptions shape the world we live in and we possess the ability to alter our perceptions today, not tomorrow. This means we hold the power to modify our actions.

As human beings, we often find ourselves in a state of constant anticipation, waiting for the "perfect time" to pursue our dreams. However, it's important to recognise that there will never be an ideal moment to start. The truth is that the perfect time is always now and if we keep waiting for the right moment, we might end up missing out on what could have been.

It's easy to fall into the trap of staying in our comfort zone, but it's essential to understand that this is where our dreams go to die. To achieve our aspirations, we must be willing to take risks and jump off the ledge. It's only when we step out of our comfort zone that we give ourselves the chance to grow and achieve our goals.

In this context, it's crucial to learn how to conquer the little voice inside our heads that tells us we can't do it. Instead of negotiating with our minds, we should learn to ignore that voice and focus on our goals. By doing this, we can smash the little voice inside our head and move towards the life we truly desire.

We must recognise that everything we want, the life we desire, is on the other side of our fears. The fear that the little voice brings up inside our heads can hold us back from the perfect version of our lives. The only way to get to the other side of fear is to step out of our comfort zone and take action.

It's easy to be held back by our fears, but we must remember that fear is the only thing we should fear. Living a life held captive by fear and staying inside our comfort zone is not a life fully lived. The only thing that should scare us is not living a life fully lived and not doing enough to make our lives and the world a better place.

We all have that little voice inside us that either acts as our biggest fan or our biggest critic. For most of us, it's the latter. We need to learn to ignore that voice and recognise that we are enough, we are worthy of success and we are capable of achieving our goals.

The perfect time to pursue our dreams is always now. We must be willing to step out of our comfort zone, conquer the little voice inside our heads and take action. The only thing we should fear is fear itself and by overcoming it, we can create the perfect version of our lives. So let's all step out of our comfort zones, take risks and achieve our goals.

Learning to overcome the little voice inside your head can be challenging. Many times, when we're about to do something, a little voice pops up and convinces us otherwise. It can tell us we don't need to complete a task now, that we can do it later, or that we shouldn't do it at all. This inner voice can be convincing and it's easy to fall into the trap of listening to it. However, if you want to succeed in life, you need to learn to go against this voice and go full force towards your goals.

If the small voice in your mind advises against doing something, take it as a signal to do the opposite. For instance, if it tells you not to love someone wholeheartedly because you're afraid of being hurt again, you should go ahead and love hard. If it tells you not to work out, then you need to work out even harder. The only way to overcome the voice is to face it head-on. By doing what it says not to, you'll be able to break free from its hold on you.

Mother Teresa is a beacon of courage, which proved that the little voice inside one's head can be silenced by taking bold steps. When she heard the voice whispering to her that it was impossible to care for the sick and dying on the streets of Calcutta, she did not give up. Instead, she took the opposite action and opened a home for the destitute and dying. She did not stop there; despite the challenges she faced, the voice inside her head telling her to give up, she continued to love the unlovable, care for the forgotten and comfort the dying. She worked tirelessly, tirelessly, dedicating her life to serving the poor and needy. Her unwavering faith and unwavering determination were a testament to the power of overcoming the voice inside one's head. By doing the opposite of what it tells us, we too can break free from its grip, just as Mother Teresa did.

In the land of Zimbabwe, where the sun beats down with relentless force and the hardships of life can weigh heavily on one's spirit, there once lived a man named Jairos Jiri. Despite being born with a physical disability, Jairos refused to let his circumstances dictate his life. When the little voice inside his head whispered that he couldn't achieve his dreams of creating a school for disabled children, he ignored it and pressed on. He worked tirelessly to turn his dream into a reality and soon, the Jairos Jiri Association was born, providing education and support to disabled children across Zimbabwe.

But Jairos' battle against the little voice inside his head didn't end there. When it whispered that he couldn't expand the association to reach even more children in need, he pushed harder, travelling to remote villages to offer education and care. And when it told him that he couldn't do more to help those suffering from the devastating effects of poverty and disease, he founded clinics and programmes to provide vital medical care and support.

Through his unwavering determination, Jairos Jiri showed us the power of the words, "It's possible" and of ignoring the little voice that tells us we can't and of taking action even when it's difficult or scary. He proved that in the face of adversity, we can choose to love wholeheartedly, to work harder and to break free from the voice that seeks to hold us back. We can do so by changing our paradigm. In doing so, he left a legacy that continues to inspire and uplift those who face their own battles today.

It's important to realise that your mind is wired to keep you safe. This is a good thing, but it can also be limiting. If you allow your mind to dictate your actions, you'll never reach your full potential. You need to take control of your thoughts and actions and overcome the little voice that holds you back.

Whenever the little voice inside your head tells you that you're not good enough, smart enough, or pretty enough, you need to combat those thoughts. Instead, focus on your strengths and what you're good at. Tell yourself that you are good enough, smart enough and pretty enough. Don't negotiate with your mind, as it can lead you down a path of self-doubt and insecurity.

Remember, the only way out is through defeating that little voice inside your brain telling you that you can't do it. You need to go against the little voice and take action. If it tells you to go back to sleep, wake up and start your day. If it tells you not to make the bed, make it. If it tells you not to make cold calls, pick up the phone and start dialling. The more you do this, the easier it will become and you'll start to see the results you want.

Learning to overcome the little "reptilian" voice inside your head takes practice and determination. You need to go against it and take action to break free from its hold. Don't negotiate with your mind or let it dictate your actions. Take control of your thoughts and actions and you'll be able to achieve your goals.

As humans, we have a complex brain with three distinct parts: the reptilian, the limbic and the neocortex. The reptilian part of our brain, also known as the primitive brain, is responsible for our survival instincts and basic needs such as food, shelter and safety. However, it can also hold us back from achieving our full potential by causing us to act on instinct rather than logic. The reptilian part of your brain can slow you down, so it has to be fought so that we don't react instinctively rather than logically to issues, which can hinder our progress and success.

Bonus poem

The perfect time is now, don't wait for tomorrow

For the present is a gift, don't waste it in sorrow
Opportunity knocks, seize it with your might
For time is precious, it can't be won by a fight

Yesterday is gone and tomorrow is yet to come
Today is all we have, make the most of it, don't succumb
To fears or doubts, let courage guide your way
Believe in yourself and let your dreams have a say

The perfect time is now, so don't hesitate
Take the first step, don't let fear be your fate
Embrace the journey, for it is what makes us grow
And remember, every success starts with a "Go".

Chapter 13 – The Power of Momentum

Don't underestimate the power of momentum. It can turn your dreams into reality and take you places you never thought possible.

Momentum is the engine that drives progress. Start small, build momentum and soon you'll be making leaps and bounds towards your goals.

Success is not a one-time event, but a series of small wins that build upon each other. The key is to keep moving forward, even if progress seems slow. Because once you gain momentum, anything is possible. - Mel Robbins

Have you ever noticed how some people seem to effortlessly achieve their goals while others struggle to make progress? It's not luck or innate talent that sets successful people apart. It's momentum. People who succeed have momentum, a driving force that propels them forward and gives them the energy and determination to keep going, even when faced with obstacles and setbacks.

Momentum is the force that propels an object in motion. In the context of success, momentum refers to the energy and forward motion that drives people to achieve their goals. When you have momentum, you feel like you're making progress and that progress gives you the motivation to keep going.

Momentum is like a snowball rolling downhill. At first, it's small and slow-moving, but as it picks up speed, it grows larger and more powerful. The same is true for momentum in your life. As you make progress towards your goals, you build momentum, which in turn makes it easier to keep making progress.

There are many real life examples of people who succeeded with momentum. Oprah Winfrey is one of the most successful women in the world, with a net worth of over $2.6 billion. But Oprah didn't start out with money or connections. She grew up in poverty and faced numerous challenges on her path to success.

What set Oprah apart was her relentless drive and determination. She knew what she wanted and was willing to work hard to get it. She started as a local news anchor, but her natural charisma and talent soon landed her a national talk show. From there, she launched her own media empire, including a magazine, a television network and a production company.

Oprah's success is a testament to the power of momentum. She started small, but as she made progress, she built momentum, which propelled her to even greater heights of success.

Elon Musk is another example of someone who has harnessed the power of momentum to achieve great things. Musk is the founder of several successful companies, including Tesla, SpaceX and PayPal.

Musk's success is due in part to his ability to set audacious goals and then relentlessly pursue them. He has a reputation for being a workaholic, often putting in 80-100 hour workweeks to achieve his goals. But Musk's success isn't just due to hard work. He also knows how to build momentum. For example, when he launched Tesla, he didn't start out with a fully electric car. Instead, he started with a high-end sports car, which helped him build momentum and credibility in the automotive industry. From there, he was able to use that momentum to launch more affordable electric cars and eventually become the leader in the electric vehicle market.

J.K. Rowling is one of the most successful authors in history, with over 500 million books sold worldwide. But Rowling's success didn't come easily. She faced numerous rejections before finally finding a publisher for her first book, Harry Potter and the Philosopher's Stone. What set Rowling apart was her unwavering belief in herself and her story.

Despite facing rejection after rejection, Rowling never gave up on her dream of becoming a published author. She kept writing and submitting her manuscript, even when it seemed like no one wanted to read it. When she finally did get a publisher, the momentum of her success was unstoppable. The Harry Potter series became a cultural phenomenon, with millions of fans around the world. Rowling's success didn't stop there. She went on to write other successful books and become a philanthropist, donating millions of dollars to charity.

Rowling's story is a testament to the power of momentum. She kept pushing forward, even when it seemed like she would never achieve her dreams. But as she made progress and built momentum, success became inevitable.

By focusing on small steps and building on your successes, you can create a powerful force that propels you towards your desired outcome. Remember, success is not a one-time event; it's a series of consistent actions taken over time. So, whether you're trying to start a business, write a book, or learn a new skill, remember that momentum is key. Start small, build on your successes and keep going, even when it gets tough. Surround yourself with supportive people who believe in you and don't be afraid to ask for help when you need it.

At its core, momentum is simply the power of movement and a leader's best friend. Sometimes it's the only difference between winning and losing. John Maxwell boldly stated that, "Momentum solves 80 percent of your problems." This is because when we take action towards our goals, we create momentum that helps us to keep moving forward even when faced with obstacles or setbacks. We are in a state of flow and everything seems to come easier. Our focus is sharp, our energy is high and we are motivated to take action towards our goals. With this momentum, we can overcome obstacles that once seemed insurmountable and we can make progress towards our objectives.

One of the most powerful aspects of momentum is that it creates a positive feedback loop. As we make progress towards our goals, we build confidence, motivation and a sense of momentum that helps us to tackle even bigger challenges. This positive cycle of growth and success can be incredibly energising and rewarding and can help us to achieve things we never thought possible by changing our paradigm.

Of course, building momentum isn't always easy. It requires us to take consistent action towards our goals, even when we don't feel like it or when things get tough. But with practice and determination, we can learn to harness the power of momentum and use it to achieve our wildest dreams.

Whether we're starting a new business, pursuing a new career path, or working towards personal growth and self-improvement, the power of momentum can be a game-changer. By taking consistent action towards our goals, building positive habits and routines and surrounding ourselves with supportive people and resources, we can create a sense of momentum that helps us to overcome challenges, build confidence and achieve our dreams.

So if you're feeling stuck or stagnant in your life, remember the power of momentum. Take action towards your goals, even if it's just a small step and keep moving forward. With time, effort and persistence, you can create a powerful momentum that can help you to achieve success in all areas of your life.

Bonus poem

The power of momentum,
Is like a force unbroken,
A strength that builds with time,
And keeps us moving forward with every climb.

It starts with a single step,
And grows with every stride,
Pushing us to greater heights,
And never letting us hide.

The power of momentum,
Is a force to be reckoned with,
It propels us towards our goals,
And never lets us quit.

So take that first step forward,
And let the momentum guide your way,
With determination and perseverance,
Success will surely come your way.

Chapter 14 – Fear Is a Great Motivator

Fear keeps us focused on the past or worried about the future. If we can acknowledge our fear, we can realise that right now we are okay. Right now, today, we are still alive and our bodies are working marvellously. Our eyes can still see the beautiful sky. Our ears can still hear the voices of our loved ones. - Thich Nhat Hanh

He who has overcome his fears will truly be free. - Aristotle

Why do some people overcome incredible obstacles, fail many times or defy grim odds in order to succeed and others simply fail? It is because of fear. Fear and resistance can hold us back from taking the necessary steps towards a better future or fulfilling a life-long dream.

But fear doesn't have to be our enemy. In fact, it can be a powerful motivator. By acknowledging our fears and learning to overcome them, we can use them as fuel for making progress towards our goals. This is where the power of a growth mindset comes in.

A growth mindset is the belief that our abilities and intelligence can be developed through hard work, dedication and perseverance. Instead of seeing challenges and failures as setbacks, those with a growth mindset view them as opportunities for growth and learning. With a growth mindset, we can turn our fears and resistance into stepping stones towards success.

When I was growing up, my greatest fear was not a fear of heights or the horror films I saw on TV, but rather the fear of day-to-day life itself. I wasn't always an anxious person, but in my teen years – and my family didn't know this – I was constantly worried about the "what ifs" in life. What if mum dies? What if I fail my exams? What if I don't get a good job? This fear prevented me from seizing opportunities that may not come my way again. Even before I knew what "anxiety" meant, I was consumed by it every second of every day of my teen years.

I believed that I would always feel this way. - afraid and alone - and that change was impossible because anxious thoughts had become my default state.

As I progressed through school and university, my fear grew to the point where it affected my confidence and self-esteem. One day, I decided I had had enough. I knew I needed to change, but I didn't know how.

My greatest fear was living a life of anxiety and depression and that fear was motivation enough for me to make a change. I realised I had two options: continue to be depressed and fearful or use my fear to motivate me. After nearly a decade of anxiety, I had reached a critical mass where I no longer cared about feeling exposed or foolish. I was determined to overcome my fear and I knew I had to take action.

Reaching this critical point in my life allowed me to gain perspective on my situation. I focused on productive activities and took risks to pursue my passions. I read many self-help books and started applying for jobs that could earn me money. I wanted to leave my country of origin and go to faraway places where I could start life afresh. As a result, I started to feel mentally free.

I learned that most people are afraid of being judged by others, which prevents them from pursuing their dreams. By overcoming my own fear, I was able to gain a new sense of confidence and freedom.

If you are struggling with anxiety or fear, I encourage you to take a step back and gain perspective on your situation. Don't let fear prevent you from living the life you truly want.

When we face fear and resistance, it's easy to give in and let them hold us back from achieving our goals. But the truth is, fear and resistance are actually indicators that we are stepping outside of our comfort zone and growing as individuals. By acknowledging our fears and resistance and reframing them as opportunities for growth, we can use them as fuel to propel us forward instead of holding us back. Soon enough, we will have the determination to achieve what we feared at first.

Sports are a great example of how fear and determination can play a significant role in achieving success. Athletes face fear and uncertainty every day, whether it's before a big game or competition or during training sessions.

One example of fear and determination in sports is the story of Michael Jordan. Despite his incredible talent and success, Jordan faced numerous setbacks and failures throughout his career. However, he never gave up and continued to work hard to improve his game. He used his fear of failure as motivation and determination to become the best basketball player in the world. His determination and fearlessness helped him win six NBA championships and earn countless awards and accolades.

Another example is the story of Simone Biles, the most decorated gymnast in history. She faced many obstacles and injuries throughout her career, but she never let fear hold her back. Instead, she used her fear to drive her to work harder and overcome her challenges. Her determination and focus helped her win 25 Olympic and World Championship medals, making her one of the most successful gymnasts of all time.

Usain Bolt is still the fastest man in the world. Bolt faced significant fear and pressure before every race, but he always remained determined and focused on his goal. He used his fear as fuel to drive him to work harder and faster and it paid off as he won nine Olympic gold medals and broke numerous world records.

Outside of sports, we have the example of Malala Yousafzai, a young girl from Pakistan who was shot by the Taliban for advocating for girls' education. Despite the danger and fear she faced, Malala remained determined to fight for what she believed in. She went on to become a powerful advocate for girls' education and was awarded the Nobel Peace Prize for her work. Today, Malala continues to inspire people around the world with her courage and determination.

These examples shows us that fear and determination are both powerful forces that can shape our lives in significant ways. While fear can hold us back, determination can help us overcome our fears and achieve great things. Whether it's pursuing a dream career, starting a business, or fighting for a cause we believe in, it's important to cultivate determination and use it to push past our fears and achieve our goals.

Embrace a growth mindset and view challenges and failures as opportunities for learning and growth. Believe in yourself and your abilities to overcome obstacles and achieve your goals. Remember, every successful person has faced fear and resistance at some point, but it's their ability to push past these obstacles with determination that sets them apart.

So how do we overcome our fears and resistance? The first step is to identify them. What is holding you back from making the changes you want to see in your life? Is it fear of failure? Fear of the unknown? Fear of judgment from others? Once you have identified your fears, you can begin to tackle them head-on.

One effective way to overcome fear is to break it down into smaller, more manageable steps. Instead of focusing on the big, daunting goal, focus on the smaller steps that will get you there. Celebrate each small victory along the way and use them as motivation to keep going.

Another way to overcome fear and resistance is to surround yourself with supportive people who believe in you and your goals. Seek out mentors, friends, or family members who will encourage and uplift you as you work towards your dreams.
And finally, remember that failure is not the end of the road. It's a natural part of the learning process and it's how we grow and develop our skills. With a growth mindset, we can embrace failures as opportunities to learn and improve, rather than as evidence of our limitations.

Imagine you have always dreamed of starting your own business. You have a great idea, but the thought of taking that leap of faith fills you with fear and anxiety. You worry about failure, financial ruin and what others might think of you if you don't succeed.

It's important to acknowledge these fears and understand that they are a natural part of the process. However, it's also important to not let them hold you back from pursuing your dreams. The key is to shift your mindset from one of fear and resistance to one of growth and possibility.

Start by identifying the specific fears and resistance that are holding you back. Write them down and examine them objectively. Are they valid concerns or are they based on limiting beliefs and self-doubt?

Once you have identified these fears, take small steps towards facing them. For example, if you are afraid of failure, start by setting small goals and celebrating each achievement. If you are worried about financial ruin, create a detailed plan and budget for your business and seek out advice from experts in the field.

By overcoming fear and resistance, you open yourself up to new possibilities and opportunities. You may even discover strengths and talents you never knew you had. So don't let fear hold you back from pursuing your dreams. Embrace the power of a growth mindset and take those small steps towards making your goals a reality.

Bonus poem

Fear can be a powerful force,
Pushing us to take a different course.
It can make us run or make us freeze,
But it can also bring us to our knees.

For fear can be a great motivator,
Driving us to become something greater.
It can light a fire deep within,
Pushing us to strive and never give in.

So let fear be a guide, but not a chain,
Use it to propel you forward, not restrain.
Let it be the wind beneath your wings,
And see the amazing things that it brings.

Chapter 15 – Love and Paradigm Shift

"Be willing to go all out, in pursuit of your dream. Ultimately it will pay off. You are more powerful than you think you are. Go for it". - Les Brown

Love has the power to transform our entire paradigm of existence. It can shatter our preconceived notions and limiting beliefs, opening up a world of new and exciting possibilities.

There was once a man who had grown up in a rough neighbourhood in Dar es Salaam, Tanzania. Despite the odds against him, he worked hard to create a better life for himself. He became a successful businessman and was admired by many for his hard work and determination.

But deep down, the man felt like something was missing. He had never found true love and he felt like he was living a life without purpose. That's when he met a woman from Zanzibar who changed everything. The man and the woman fell in love and they built a life together that was based on mutual respect, admiration and a shared desire to make a positive impact on the world.

The woman saw the man's potential and encouraged him to think beyond his current circumstances. With her support, the man's paradigm shifted. He began to see the world in a new light and he realised that there was more to life than just success and material possessions.

Together, they started a charity called "Watoto wa Tumaini", a Swahili name loosely translated to "Children of Hope". The charity was a huge success and the man and the woman became known for their philanthropic work. They inspired others to join their cause and together, they were able to create a better world for those who needed it most.

Today the charity provides education and support to over 50,000 underprivileged children in East Africa. The man's perspective had shifted and he was no longer just focused on his own success. He had discovered the joy of giving back and making a difference in the lives of others.

In Cochabamba, Bolivia, a story is told of a young couple that was deeply in love, but they were faced with a daunting challenge. The young man, Carlos, was a great cueca dancer. Cueca is the national dance of Bolivia that involves a couple's dance with flirtatious movements. Carlos had been in a terrible accident that left him paralysed from the waist down. Doctors had told him that he would never walk again.

Despite the bleak prognosis, his girlfriend, Marcela, refused to give up on him. She was determined to help him regain his mobility and together they started an intense physical therapy regimen.

The first few weeks were difficult and progress was slow. Carlos often felt discouraged and hopeless, but Marcela refused to let him give up. She encouraged him to keep pushing and reminded him of the love they shared.

Over time, Carlos began to notice small improvements. He could move his toes and slowly started to regain some sensation in his legs. This gave him hope and motivated him to work even harder.

One day, as Carlos was doing his exercises, he suddenly felt a jolt in his legs. It was like nothing he had felt before. He looked at Marcela, who was grinning from ear to ear. She had been secretly working with the physical therapist to develop a new exercise that would help Carlos regain the use of his legs.

From that moment on, Carlos's progress was rapid. He was able to stand, take a few steps and eventually even walk again and dance his cueca dance. It was a paradigm shift for Carlos, who had been told he would never walk again.

Throughout it all, Marcela remained his rock, encouraging him, loving him and supporting him every step of the way. Their love had helped them overcome an incredible challenge and had taught them the power of hope, perseverance and the willingness to embrace a new way of thinking. Carlos and Marcela knew that their love had helped them overcome the odds and they were filled with gratitude for each other and the journey they had shared.

These true stories are powerful reminders that love can transform our lives in ways we never thought possible. When we find someone who believes in us and supports us, we can achieve great things and make a real difference in the world. By shifting our paradigms and opening ourselves up to new experiences and perspectives, we can discover our true purpose and live a life filled with joy and meaning.

Love has the power to shift our paradigms, to open our minds and hearts to new perspectives and to inspire us to persevere through any challenge. When we shift our mindset to one of love, hope and perseverance, we can overcome even the most difficult obstacles.

Let us remember that love is not just a feeling, but a powerful force that can drive us to take action and make a difference in the world. When we choose to act with love, we bring light to the darkest of situations and can inspire others to do the same. We must never underestimate the power of love and its ability to bring about positive change in our lives and in the lives of those around us.

In times of adversity, it can be easy to give up and lose hope. However, when we cultivate a mindset of love, hope and perseverance, we can find the strength to keep going, even when the road ahead seems uncertain. Love gives us the courage to face our fears and the determination to overcome them. It creates a ripple effect of positivity that can transform the world and can transform our entire paradigm of existence. It can shatter our preconceived notions and limiting beliefs, opening up a world of new and exciting possibilities.

Bonus poem

Love and paradigm shift,
Two forces that can lift,
The heart and mind to new heights,
Unleashing potential, igniting new lights.

Love opens up the soul,
A force that can make one whole,
Paradigm shift brings a new view,
The old way fades and the new comes through.

Together they bring a powerful force,
Unlocking new doors, setting new course,
For a life full of passion and purpose,
Where love and paradigm shift find their nexus.

Chapter 16 – Changing Your Mindset

"Change the way you look at things and the things you look at change.". - Wayne Dyer

Changing your mindset is not a one-time event, it's a daily practice.

Changing your mindset can be a powerful tool for achieving immeasurable success in life. Adopting a growth mindset can help us overcome obstacles and achieve our goals. By shifting from a fixed mindset to a growth mindset, we can develop a sense of resilience and learn to see challenges as opportunities for growth. You can alter your life by altering your attitude to challenges and view yourself as invincible. This is the greatest agent and catalyst for change.

Through self-awareness and a willingness to learn, we can begin to identify and challenge our limiting beliefs and negative thought patterns. By embracing a growth mindset, we can cultivate a sense of curiosity and openness to new experiences, which can lead to greater creativity and innovation.

Mother Teresa is an inspiring example of someone who shifted her mindset to create immense positive change in the world. She was born in Albania and initially joined a convent at the age of 18, but it wasn't until later in life that she truly embraced her calling to help the poor and sick.

Mother Teresa's mindset shifted from a focus on personal achievement and success to a focus on selfless service to others. She saw the suffering of the poorest of the poor in Calcutta, India and realised that she had to do something to help them. She founded the Missionaries of Charity, an organisation dedicated to caring for the sick, the dying and the destitute.

Despite the enormous challenges she faced in her work, including criticism and scepticism from some quarters, Mother Teresa persevered. She remained focused on her mission and worked tirelessly to help those in need. She became an icon of compassion and service, inspiring people all over the world to follow her example and make a difference in their own communities.

Mother Teresa's example shows us that shifting our mindset can lead to extraordinary results. When we focus on the needs of others and commit ourselves to a higher purpose, we can achieve great things and create lasting positive change in the world.

One inspiring example of a person who shifted their mindset and achieved success despite physical limitations is the story of Sudha Chandran, an Indian classical dancer. At the age of 16, Sudha lost her right leg in a car accident, which ended her dreams of becoming a professional dancer. However, instead of giving up on her passion, Sudha made the decision to shift her mindset and overcome her physical limitations.

She started to use a prosthetic leg and went on to train hard and perfect her art. Despite the challenges, Sudha refused to let her disability define her and instead, she used it as a motivation to push herself further. Her hard work and determination paid off and she went on to become a world-renowned classical dancer, receiving numerous accolades and awards for her performances.

Sudha's story is a true testament to the power of a growth mindset and the determination to overcome challenges. She serves as an inspiration to anyone facing adversity and a reminder that with the right mindset and attitude, anything is possible.

Nelson Mandela, despite facing years of imprisonment and being labelled a terrorist by the apartheid government in South Africa, never lost hope or gave up on his dream of a free and democratic South Africa.

During his imprisonment, Mandela educated himself and learned to see the bigger picture beyond his personal struggles. He embraced the philosophy of nonviolence and reconciliation, which became the cornerstone of his leadership style. When he was finally released from prison after 27 years, he did not seek revenge or retribution but instead worked towards a peaceful transition to democracy in South Africa.

Mandela's transformation from a militant activist to a statesman and peacemaker was a testament to his growth mindset. He was able to adapt to changing circumstances, learn from his experiences and embrace new ideas and approaches. Through his perseverance, determination and willingness to change his mindset, Mandela inspired millions of people around the world and left a lasting legacy of hope, forgiveness and reconciliation.

Finally, an example of a child who achieved great success through a mindset shift is that of Ryan Hreljac. At the age of just six years old he learned about the lack of access to clean water in many parts of the world. Instead of feeling helpless, Ryan decided to take action and started fundraising to build a well in a Ugandan village. Since then, Ryan has founded his own non-profit organisation, Ryan's Well Foundation, which has provided clean water and sanitation to over 10 million people in developing countries.

Mindset shifting has the power to transform our perception of the world and our ability to achieve success. By changing our mindset and adopting a more positive and proactive approach to life, we can create new opportunities, overcome obstacles and reach our full potential. We have the power to control our own perspective and create the reality we desire.

Remember, your mindset is a powerful tool that can either hold you back or propel you forward towards success. By shifting your mindset to focus on growth, positivity and possibility, you can overcome obstacles, embrace challenges and achieve your goals. As the famous quote by Henry Ford goes, "Whether you think you can, or you think you can't. - you're right." So choose to believe in yourself, your abilities and your potential and watch as your mindset helps you achieve immeasurable success.

You have the power to change your mindset and create the life you want. It may not be easy and it may take time, but with determination, perseverance and a willingness to learn and grow, anything is possible. Keep pushing forward and don't be afraid to seek support from others who can help you along the way. By shifting your mindset, you can unlock a world of possibilities and achieve success beyond your wildest dreams. So don't let fear or self-doubt hold you back - take that first step towards a positive mindset today and see where it takes you.

Bonus poem

From limiting beliefs, we must break free
And open up to new possibilities we cannot yet see
For the mind is powerful, but also can be trapped
By negative thoughts and beliefs that need to be scrapped

Changing your mindset, it's no easy feat
But it's worth the effort to make life complete
Focus on the positive and let go of the past
The possibilities are endless, your future is vast

Believe in yourself and all you can do
And your mindset will shift, to a world that is new
Where opportunities abound and happiness reigns
And your life will be filled, with endless gains.

Chapter 17 – Building Positive Habits

"Success is not final, failure is not fatal: it is the courage to continue that counts.". - Winston Churchill

As human beings, we are creatures of habit. Our daily routines and habits shape who we are and what we can achieve. Habits are the foundation of our lives and they can be either good or bad. Building positive habits is essential to achieving our goals and living a fulfilled life. However, developing positive habits takes courage and perseverance. It's not always easy to stick to your habits, but it's important to keep going, even when you face setbacks or obstacles.

Habits are the automatic behaviours that we perform every day. These behaviours are deeply ingrained in our brains and are difficult to change. When we try to change a habit, our brains resist the change, making it challenging to create new habits or break old ones.

However, if we can harness the power of habits, we can use them to our advantage. Positive habits can help us achieve our goals and live a healthier and more fulfilling life. Positive habits such as exercising, eating healthy and practicing mindfulness can lead to improved physical and mental health. They are small, everyday actions that can have a big impact on our lives and help us develop the skills and mindset we need to succeed in our personal and professional lives.

Motivational speaker Anthony Robbins says, "It's not what we do once in a while that shapes our lives. It's what we do consistently." Consistency is key when it comes to building positive habits. It's the actions you take consistently that will have the greatest impact on your life, not the one-off giant steps that you take.

Positive habits are not just theoretical concepts; they are practical actions that can lead to real-life success. Many women have achieved great things by adopting positive habits and integrating them into their daily lives. Sheryl Sandberg, the COO of Facebook, is a successful businesswoman and advocate for women in leadership positions. She is known for her efficient use of time and productivity. Sheryl is a proponent of prioritising tasks and focusing on the most important ones first, which allows her to accomplish more in less time.

Sara Blakely is the founder of Spanx, a successful shapewear company. She is known for her resilience and positive attitude towards failure. Sara sees failure as an opportunity to learn and grow and she uses her failures as motivation to keep pushing forward.

These women are just a few examples of how building positive habits can lead to success in various areas of life. By adopting positive habits and making them a part of your daily routine, you can also achieve great things and live the life you want to live.

Positive habits are the key to unlocking a fulfilling and happy life. Habits are powerful because they shape our thoughts, actions and ultimately our destiny. By consciously cultivating positive habits, you can create a life filled with joy, purpose and success.

One of the most compelling reasons to develop positive habits is that they help you achieve your goals. When you have a clear vision of what you want to achieve and you consistently engage in habits that support that vision, you increase your chances of success. Habits are like building blocks that slowly but surely create the foundation for your desired outcome.

Building positive habits is not about being perfect. It's about progress, not perfection. Every small step that you take towards your goal is a step in the right direction. Even if you stumble along the way, don't give up. Every day is a new opportunity to start fresh and recommit to your positive habits.

One of the most inspiring things about positive habits is that they are cumulative. Each day that you engage in a positive habit, you strengthen your resolve and commitment to that habit. Over time, these small steps can lead to incredible transformations in your life.

Positive habits also improve your overall well-being. Habits like regular exercise, healthy eating and mindfulness meditation have been shown to reduce stress, increase happiness and boost productivity. When you take care of yourself in this way, you create a positive feedback loop that strengthens your mental and physical resilience.

Kobe Bryant. - the late NBA superstar was known for his legendary work ethic, which he attributed to his daily habits. He would wake up at 4am every day to work out and practice and would continue to train and practice throughout the day. His dedication to his craft and commitment to his daily habits helped him become one of the greatest basketball players of all time.

Another benefit of positive habits is that they can transform your mindset. Habits like daily affirmations, gratitude journaling and positive self-talk help you cultivate a positive attitude and outlook on life. This can have a profound impact on your mental health, relationships and overall sense of purpose.

Finally, positive habits help you create a life of meaning and significance. When you engage in habits that align with your values and beliefs, you create a sense of purpose and fulfilment. Whether it's practicing kindness or pursuing a passion project or profession, positive habits can help you create a life that feels truly meaningful.

Denzel Washington, the renowned actor and director, is known for his positive mindset and commitment to developing good habits. Some of the positive habits and mindset he embodies are consistency, perseverance, gratitude, positive mindset and lifelong learning. He says, "Without commitment, you'll never start, but more importantly, without consistency, you'll never finish." He is a firm believer in the power of perseverance, believing that success comes to those who are willing to work hard and never give up, even in the face of obstacles. Denzel's positive habits and mindset are an inspiration to many and serve as a reminder that success is achievable with hard work, consistency and a positive attitude.

Lastly, the power of positive habits cannot be overstated. By consciously cultivating habits that support your goals, well-being, mindset and sense of purpose, you can create a life filled with joy, fulfilment and success. So take the first step today and start building positive habits that will transform your life for the better!

Bonus poem

Building positive habits,
Is the way to win life's habits,
For every day that you live,
New habits must be actively sought and sieved.

A positive habit forms a strong base,
On which you can build and embrace,
It takes effort, time and patience,
But the results are pure brilliance.

It's all about small changes day by day,
Creating routines that pave the way,
So stay committed and stay true,
Building positive habits will see you through.

Chapter 18 – Finding Your Purpose

Your purpose is not something to be found, it is something to be created.

"When you discover your purpose and put your heart and soul into it, you will live a life of great significance. - Robin Sharma

Have you ever felt like something is missing in your life? Do you often find yourself wondering what your purpose is and why you're here? If so, you're not alone. Many people go through life without a clear sense of direction or purpose, which can leave them feeling unfulfilled and unhappy.

However, the good news is that you can change that by living a purposeful life. Living a purposeful life means discovering your passions, setting meaningful goals and making a positive impact on the world. By doing so, you can find happiness, fulfilment and success in all areas of your life.

Growing up, I always admired my mother for her strength, resilience and kindness. She was a true role model and I looked up to her in every way. But as I got older, I began to appreciate her even more when I saw how she lived a purpose-driven life.

My mother grew up with limited opportunities, but she was determined to make the most of what she had. She worked hard in school, but there were very limited opportunities for women during colonial Rhodesia. But she always felt like there was something missing.

It wasn't until she was in her late 20s that she discovered her purpose. She had always been passionate about helping others, but she wasn't sure how to turn that passion into action. Then, she started working as an auxiliary nurse for the Red Cross and it changed her life. She was happy saving lives and helping the sick and frail.

Once my mother found her purpose, she lived with passion and compassion. She devoted her time and energy to making a positive impact on the small world around her.

But it wasn't just about the actions she took. It was the way she did it. My mother had a heart full of compassion and she treated everyone with kindness and respect. She saw the best in people, even when they didn't see it in themselves. And that made a difference. Her purpose-driven life had a ripple effect on the world around her. She made a positive impact on the lives of so many people, whether it was through working, volunteering, supporting relatives or simply showing kindness and compassion.

But it wasn't just about the impact she made on others. It was the impact it had on her. She found a sense of fulfilment and meaning that she had been missing and it gave her a sense of purpose and direction. This taught me so much about living with passion and compassion.

I learnt that one has to discover their purpose. Finding your purpose is key to living a purpose-driven life. It's about aligning your values and passions with your actions and finding a sense of fulfilment and meaning. I also learnt that you have to live with passion and compassion by devoting your time and energy to making a positive impact on the world around you. It's about treating everyone with kindness and respect and seeing the best in people. Making a positive impact on the world is the ultimate goal of living a purpose-driven life.

Discovering our purpose in life is essential for leading a fulfilling and meaningful existence. Our purpose provides us with direction and motivation to pursue our goals and make positive changes in our lives. In this chapter, we will explore the importance of finding our purpose and how to align our actions with our purpose.

Many people struggle with finding their purpose, but it's important to remember that purpose is not something that is simply found; it's something that is cultivated over time. One way to start discovering your purpose is to ask yourself what brings you joy and fulfilment. What are your passions and interests? What activities make you lose track of time? What are you naturally good at? These questions can help you identify your unique gifts and talents and how they can be used to make a positive impact in the world.

Another method for discovering your purpose is to reflect on your life experiences and the lessons you've learned along the way. What challenges have you faced and overcome? What experiences have shaped your values and beliefs? What have been your greatest achievements? These reflections can help you gain clarity about what you value and what drives you.

Once you've discovered your purpose, it's important to align your goals and actions with your purpose. This means setting goals that are in line with your purpose and taking actions that support those goals. When you're clear on your purpose, you'll find that making decisions becomes easier and you'll be more motivated to take action towards your goals.

Acting is often seen as a glamorous profession, with fame, fortune and adoration from fans. However, for some actors, the pursuit of these things is not enough. They seek a deeper sense of purpose, a greater connection to the world around them and a way to make a positive impact on the world.

An inspiring example that success is not just about achieving fame and fortune but about finding meaning and making a positive impact on the world is that of Lupita Nyong'o. She is a talented Oscar-holding actress, but she's also a strong advocate for diversity and representation in the entertainment industry. She's spoken out about the importance of seeing diverse stories and perspectives on screen and has worked to empower young women and girls through education and mentorship.

Lupita found her passion for causes that are important to her and we can do the same. By exploring our interests and values, we can discover our own passions and find ways to make a positive impact on the world. She has a platform to reach a wide audience and uses that platform to raise awareness and advocate for causes she believes in.

Angelina Jolie is known for her work as an actress, but she's also an advocate for human rights and social justice. She's a special envoy for the United Nations Refugee Agency and has travelled around the world to raise awareness about refugee issues. She's also a passionate advocate for women's rights and has spoken out about sexual violence in conflict zones.

We may not have the same level of visibility, but we can still use our own platforms, whether it's through social media, community involvement, or personal relationships, or professions to make a positive impact and live fulfilling and purpose-driven lives.

Living a purpose-driven life has many benefits, including greater fulfilment and happiness. When we're aligned with our purpose, we feel a sense of meaning and direction in our lives. We're more likely to experience flow states, where we're fully engaged in what we're doing and lose track of time. We're also more resilient in the face of challenges because we know that we're working towards something meaningful.

In summary, discovering your purpose is an essential step towards living a fulfilling and meaningful life. By reflecting on your passions, interests, values and life experiences, you can gain clarity about your purpose and align your goals and actions with it. Living a purpose-driven life can lead to greater happiness, fulfilment and resilience in the face of challenges.

Bonus poem

In the depths of our being,
Lies a purpose worth freeing.
It's a flame that burns bright,
Guiding us towards the light.

It may take some time to find,
But it's always been in our mind.
A calling that stirs the soul,
A destiny that makes us whole.

The journey may be long and tough,
But the reward will be enough.

For when we align with our purpose,
We unlock a life that's truly worth it.

So let us search within and without,
For the purpose we cannot live without.
For when we find what we're meant to do,
We'll live a life that's pure and true.

Chapter 19 – Emotional Banking

Every small act of kindness towards your loved ones is a deposit into their emotional bank account, creating a foundation of love and trust that will stand the test of time.

Making a paradigm shift towards investing in emotional bank accounts is the key to building strong and fulfilling relationships.

Emotional banking is like saving up positive feelings in our hearts and minds, so we can make meaningful deposits into our relationships. It's about being kind, understanding and supportive to others, just like depositing love and care into their emotional accounts. By investing our time and energy in building strong connections, we create a rich reserve of trust, happiness and understanding. And just like a bank account, the more we invest in emotional currency, the more we can withdraw when we need it most. So let's embrace the power of emotional banking and watch our relationships flourish with love, compassion and boundless positivity.

Growing up, my father had a friend whom we simply called Mr K who had a loving wife and four beautiful children. They lived a comfortable life, but Mr K was always busy with work and didn't have much time to spend with his family. Over time, his emotional bank account with them began to dwindle.

One day, Mr K's wife fell ill and was hospitalised. As she lay in bed, Mr K realised how much he had neglected her and their family. He felt immense guilt and regret for not investing enough time and love into their relationships.

Despite the doctors' best efforts, Mr K's wife's condition worsened and she passed away. He was devastated and felt like he had lost a part of himself. He realised that he could never make up for the time he had lost with his wife and children.

But Mr K didn't give up. He took the time to grieve and reflect on his actions. He made a conscious effort to spend more quality time with his children, to listen to them and to show them love and affection. Over time, his emotional bank account with them began to grow and he could see the positive impact it had on their relationships.

Although Mr K could never bring back his wife, he found solace in knowing that he had changed his ways and made a positive difference in the lives of his children. He learned the hard way that emotional banking is a powerful force and investing in our relationships is something we should never take for granted.

Emotional banking is about investing in the people around us, building strong relationships and creating a positive impact in their lives. It's a powerful tool for personal growth and transformation, as it helps us shift our paradigm and see the world in a new light. Making a paradigm shift towards investing in emotional bank accounts is the key to building strong and fulfilling relationships.

By making emotional deposits in the form of kindness, compassion and empathy, we can create a surplus of positivity that can change our lives and the lives of those around us. It's a simple but powerful concept that has the potential to transform our relationships, careers and overall well-being.

The key to success is to shift our mindset and start investing in others with a genuine desire to create positive change. We must let go of our negative beliefs and embrace the power of emotional banking to unlock our full potential. It may not always be easy, but the rewards are immeasurable. Shifting your focus towards emotional bank accounts can lead to a happier and more meaningful life, filled with deeper, more authentic connections.

So, let us take a moment to reflect on our emotional investments and ask ourselves, "Am I making enough deposits in the emotional bank accounts of those around me? Am I investing in myself and creating a positive shift in my own paradigm?" With a little effort and determination, we can all become emotional bankers and make a difference in the world, one investment at a time.

Mr K's story is a powerful reminder of the importance of investing in our relationships. It's never too late to make a positive change and prioritise our loved ones. Mr K's decision to reflect on his actions and make a conscious effort to improve his emotional bank account with his family is truly inspirational. Let his story be a motivation for all of us to make time for the people we love and to cherish every moment with them. Life is precious and we should never take the love and support of our loved ones for granted.

Another story that I was told by my friend Colin is about a father-son relationship. The son left Zimbabwe in 2010 seeking greener pastures in New Zealand. He soon got sucked into the fast life of Auckland and forgot about his father back in Zimbabwe.

As the years went by, the father's health began to deteriorate. The family's financial situation worsened and they struggled to make ends meet. One day, the father was rushed to Harare hospital where he was diagnosed with terminal prostate cancer. The son was devastated and felt guilty for not being there for his father when he needed him the most. Colin quickly rushed t Zimbabwe.

As the father lay on his deathbed, he called his son close and whispered in his ear, "I may not have been able to leave you with a lot of material possessions, but I have deposited love and memories into your emotional bank account. Use them wisely and they will carry you far in life."

Colin was overwhelmed with emotion and realised the truth of his father's words. He may not have had a lot of money or material possessions, but he had something far more valuable: the love and memories his father had deposited into his emotional bank account.

In the years that followed, Colin worked hard to honour his father's legacy. He pursued his education and built a successful career, but never forgot the importance of emotional banking. He made it a priority to invest in his relationships with his family and friends, depositing love and memories into their emotional bank accounts. He knew that these were the things that truly mattered in life and that they would carry him far in his journey as an immigrant.

This sad immigrant story about emotional banking reminds us that material possessions come and go, but the love and memories we invest in our relationships can last a lifetime. It teaches us that even in the darkest of times emotional banking can be a powerful force that can bring us hope, comfort and strength.

The power of emotional banking is truly remarkable. It has the ability to transform our relationships and bring immense joy and fulfilment into our lives. When we invest in positive emotions and meaningful connections, we create a strong foundation that can weather any storm. Just like money in the bank, emotional deposits build trust, understanding and love. So, let's start making deposits of kindness, appreciation and compassion. The returns we'll receive in the form of deep, meaningful connections will be priceless.

Emotional banking is a gift that keeps on giving. When we take the time to listen attentively to others and show genuine empathy, we sow seeds of connection that blossom into beautiful relationships. Small acts of kindness, like a warm smile or a thoughtful gesture, can make a significant impact. These emotional investments create a ripple effect, spreading positivity and love in our lives and the lives of those around us. Let's embrace the power of emotional banking and watch as our acts of kindness compound, enriching the world with love and happiness.

The power of emotional banking lies within each and every one of us. We have the ability to make a positive difference in someone's life, simply by being there for them and offering our support. It doesn't require great wealth or grand gestures; it's the small, heartfelt moments that matter most. So, let's be mindful of our emotional investments, depositing love, understanding and encouragement wherever we go.

Together, we can create a world filled with compassion and unity, one emotional deposit at a time.

Bonus poem

Emotions are like a bank,
Where we deposit every thought we think,
The ones that make us happy and light,
And the ones that give us a fright.

We withdraw from this bank every day,
The emotions that we need to display,
Some make us feel joy and peace,
While others make our worries increase.

So be mindful of what you deposit in this bank,
And withdraw only what you need to maintain your rank,
Emotional banking is a lifelong game,
So play it well, without any shame.

Chapter 20 – Whatever You Mismanage You Lose

"Inaction breeds doubt and fear. Action breeds confidence and courage. If you want to conquer fear, do not sit home and think about it. Go out and get busy"– Dale Carnegie

Are you tired of losing out on things you've worked hard for? Maybe you've lost your finances, your relationships or even your good health due to mismanagement. If you can relate to this, it's time for a paradigm shift.

Paulo Coelho once said, "Life has a way of testing a person's will, either by having nothing happen at all or by having everything happen at once." This rings true for a young man named Tinashe who grew up in Zimbabwe and had dreams of becoming a successful businessman.

Tinashe had always been ambitious and hardworking, but he lacked discipline when it came to looking after his health, often staying up late working and neglecting to exercise or eat properly.

Despite this, Tinashe's business was thriving and he seemed to be on the path to success. However, his recklessness caught up with him when he was involved in a serious car accident that left him hospitalised for months. His medical bills piled up and he was forced to close his business.

The crisis that Tinashe faced was a result of his mismanagement of his body. He had not taken care of himself properly and as a result, he lost everything he had worked so hard for.

This tragic story serves as a reminder that the way we manage our body can determine our success or failure. The universe will only give us what we've shown we can handle and if we receive something beyond our capabilities, it can lead to a crisis. Mismanagement causes crises, which is why a paradigm shift is essential for better management. We must learn to manage our resources wisely and make responsible choices in order to achieve our goals and avoid the pitfalls of mismanagement.

Paradigm shift is about management; management of your body, your money, your relationships, your career. When you mismanage anything, you lose it. If you do not learn to manage your things, you lose them.

The way you manage your body, money, relationships and career determines your success or failure, as we saw with the story of Tinashe. If you can't manage them properly, you'll lose them. The universe will only give you what you've shown you can handle. If you receive something beyond your capabilities, it can lead to a crisis. Mismanagement causes crises, which is why a paradigm shift is essential for better management.

To effectively manage your life, you need to start with managing your body. Jim Rohn once said, "Take care of your body, it's the only place you have to live." Your body is your vehicle to achieve your dreams and goals, so it's essential to manage it properly. Exercise, eat healthy foods, get enough sleep and avoid habits that can harm your health. By doing this, you can improve your mental and physical well-being and ultimately, your life.

According to Stephen Covey, "We see the world, not as it is, but as we are or, as we are conditioned to see it." The way you manage your life is based on your paradigms, your mindset and beliefs. If your paradigms are negative, your outcomes will be negative. But if you shift your paradigm, your life can change for the better.

Mismanagement of your finances can lead to significant losses. As financial expert "A budget is telling your money where to go instead of wondering where it went," according to Dave Ramsey ." Create a budget, invest wisely and spend less than you earn. If you can't manage your finances, you'll continue to struggle financially.

Managing your relationships is another critical aspect of your life. It's not about the number of friends you have, but the quality of the relationships you cultivate. Robin Sharma says that relationships are the bridges that lead to great things, so it is important to build healthy relationships, communicate effectively and show gratitude towards those who support you, so that they can continue to do so and you continue to learn. Change is the end result of all true learning.

To help you shift your paradigm, start by identifying the limiting beliefs and negative thought patterns that are holding you back. Then, challenge them and replace them with positive affirmations and empowering beliefs. Surround yourself with people who support and encourage you and seek out resources and tools to help you manage your life better.

Mismanagement leads to significant losses, but a paradigm shift can help you manage things better. According to American writer, Zig Ziglar, "People often say that motivation doesn't last. Well, neither does bathing, that's why we recommend it daily." Continuously work on shifting your paradigms and you'll see an improvement in your life. Start by managing your body, your money and your relationships and watch your life transform.

Bonus poem

Whatever you mismanage, you lose,
Time, money, relationships, you must choose
To nurture and cherish, to tend with care,
Or watch them slip away, leaving you in despair.

A bank account drained, with nothing to show,
A friendship neglected, that now must go,
Mismanagement leads to a life out of sync,
But with discipline and effort, you can begin to think.

To take control of your life, your assets, your fate,
To avoid the pitfalls and not be too late,
With wisdom and knowledge, your life you can choose,
To manage it well and never lose.

Chapter 21 – Never Too Late To Change Your Paradigm

Even in our darkest moments, we can find hope and meaning if we're willing to look for it.

The purpose of life is not to be happy. It is to be useful, to be honourable, to be compassionate, to have it make some difference that you have lived and lived well . - Ralph Waldo Emerson

Life can change in an instant. For US author, Craig Shapiro, it was the sudden loss of his beloved wife at the young age of 34 that transformed his life forever. He was left to raise their 10-year-old daughter alone while also grappling with the overwhelming grief and sense of purposelessness that comes with such a profound loss.

As the co-owner of a successful silkscreen business in San Francisco, Craig had been living a comfortable and contented life. However, his wife's death had shattered his world and made him question the very meaning of his existence. He knew that he needed to find a new path, a new paradigm, but he had no idea where to start.

For months, Craig wandered in a fog of grief and uncertainty, unable to find a way forward. He felt lost and alone, with no clear direction or purpose in life. But then, something remarkable happened. He began to dream.

In these dreams, Craig saw himself helping others to find joy and laughter in the midst of pain and suffering. He saw himself using humour as a powerful tool for healing and transformation. At first, he dismissed these dreams as nothing more than wishful thinking, but they persisted, night after night.

Gradually, Craig began to realise that these dreams were a message from his own subconscious, urging him to explore the healing power of humour. He started to research the topic, reading everything he could find on the subject. He also began to volunteer with people who were dying, to see firsthand how they used humour to cope with their own pain and suffering.

As he delved deeper into this world of therapeutic humour, Craig began to see a new path opening up before him. He decided to go back to school to learn more about the subject and eventually, he wrote his first book, 'The Healing Power of Humour'. Today, his book has been translated into nine different languages and he has become a leading expert in the field of therapeutic humour.

Craig's story is a powerful reminder that it's never too late to change your life or the way you see the world. This is your paradigm. No matter how old you are, or how entrenched you may feel in your current circumstances, you can always choose to chart a new course.

The key is to be open to new experiences and to be willing to take risks. It's easy to get stuck in a rut, to become complacent or resigned to a life that feels comfortable but unfulfilling. But when you're faced with a significant challenge or loss, as Craig was, it can shake you out of that complacency and force you to re-evaluate your priorities.

In Craig's case, his wife's death was a wake-up call that jolted him out of his comfortable routine and made him question everything he thought he knew about himself and his life. But instead of giving in to despair or hopelessness, he chose to use that pain as a catalyst for growth and transformation.

The key to Craig's success was his willingness to embrace a new paradigm. He could have continued down the same path he had been on, running his business and living a comfortable but unremarkable life. But instead, he chose to pursue a new passion, one that was completely outside his comfort zone.

In doing so, Craig discovered a whole new world of possibilities and opportunities. He found a sense of purpose and meaning that he had never known before and he was able to make a real difference in the lives of others.

Remember, growth is not always easy. It often requires us to step outside of our comfort zones and face our fears. But the rewards of growth are immeasurable - increased confidence, greater self-awareness and a deeper sense of purpose.
When we choose to grow through our challenges, we become the masters of our own destiny. We take control of our lives and create the future we want for ourselves. We become the architects of our own triumphs.

So if you're feeling stuck or discouraged, take heart from TD Jakes' words. Remember that change is inevitable, but growth is optional. Choose to embrace change and use it as a catalyst for personal growth. Choose to turn your tragedies into triumphs and see how far you can go

Even in the midst of darkness, there is always a glimmer of hope. Follow it and see where it leads. Sometimes, it takes a major challenge or loss to shake us out of our comfort zone and open our eyes to new possibilities. So, don't let fear or self-doubt hold you back from pursuing your passions. Believe in yourself and take that first step in changing your paradigm or the way you see the world.

When you find your purpose, it's like a light switch turning on. Suddenly, everything makes sense and you know what you need to do. Life is a journey and the path is never straight. Embrace the twists and turns and keep moving forward with faith and determination.

You, too, can find your way forward like Craig did, no matter how challenging the road may be. Remember, it's never too late to change your paradigm and pursue your dreams. Trust that with perseverance and a willingness to learn and grow, you can overcome any obstacle and achieve your goals. So go ahead, take that first step towards your dreams. And know that you have what it takes to create the life you truly desire. Believe in yourself and the rest will fall into place.

Bonus poem

The old ways may have served you well,
But now it's time to break the spell.
Change your paradigm and shift your view,
A whole new world will open up to you.

It's never too late to make a change,
To break free from habits that seem strange.
Open your mind to new possibilities,
And embrace the power of new realities.

It's never too late to break the mould,
To create a new story that's yet untold.
To let go of the past and embrace the new,
To live life on your terms and see it through.

Chapter 22 – Flawed Paradigms Lead To Flawed Decisions

It's not the strongest of the species that survives, nor the most intelligent, but the one most responsive to change. - Charles Darwin

We are what we repeatedly do. Excellence, then, is not an act, but a habit.. - Aristotle

The way we see the world shapes the way we make decisions and the actions we take. Our paradigms, or our perceptions, are shaped by our experiences, beliefs and values. More often than not, it's not our decisions that lead us astray, but our flawed paradigms. Shifting our paradigms can change our lives for the better.

The eagle is a powerful and majestic bird that can teach us a lot about shifting our paradigms. When eagles hunt, they rely on their sharp eyesight to spot their prey from afar. However, they don't just see the prey, they also see the bigger picture. They understand how the wind is blowing, where the sun is shining and how the landscape is changing. This allows them to make informed decisions and take the right actions.

In the same way, we need to see the bigger picture and shift our paradigms to make better decisions and take the right actions in our lives. Sometimes, we get so caught up in our own experiences, beliefs and values that we lose sight of the bigger picture. We make decisions based on flawed paradigms that can lead us astray.

However, if we learn to shift our paradigms and see things from different angles, we can make more informed decisions and take actions that align with our true values and goals. Just like the eagle, we need to be willing to look beyond what's right in front of us and see the bigger picture. By doing so, we can soar to new heights and achieve the success and fulfilment we desire.

Lions are often seen as powerful and ferocious predators, but their behaviour is actually shaped by their paradigms. For example, a group of lions known as the Tsavo Man-Eaters were responsible for several human deaths in Kenya in the late 19th century. At the time, the British colonial government sent two hunters to kill the lions and protect the workers building a railway.

The two hunters, Lt. Col. John Henry Patterson and his team, initially struggled to kill the lions because they were using their usual hunting methods. However, they soon realised that their paradigm of hunting big game with rifles was not going to work against these particular lions, who had become accustomed to preying on humans and would attack at night and avoid guns. The lions were able to outsmart the hunters by avoiding their traps and even attacking their camp at night.

It was only when Patterson changed his paradigm and decided to use a new method of hunting, one that involved using a large steel trap and baiting the lions with a live donkey, that they were able to finally kill the man-eaters.

The hunters also realised that the lions were targeting humans as a means of survival. Due to a combination of drought and overhunting of their natural prey, the lions had developed a new paradigm where humans were seen as a viable food source; there weren't that many animals to prey on. Once the hunters understood this paradigm shift, they were able to devise a plan to kill the lions and protect the workers.

This example shows how the way we see the world shapes our behaviour and actions. The lions' paradigm shift led to their aggressive behaviour towards humans, just as our flawed paradigms can lead us astray in our own decision-making. It's important to recognise that our perceptions and beliefs are shaped by our experiences and values and that these can be changed through new experiences and learning.

This story illustrates how even experienced hunters with a successful track record can be limited by their paradigms. It was only when they were willing to change their perspective and approach the problem from a new angle that they were able to succeed.

This is a valuable lesson that can be applied to our own lives. If we are constantly stuck in the same paradigm, we will be limited in our ability to make decisions and take actions that lead to success. But if we are willing to challenge our own paradigms and look at things from a new perspective, we can find creative solutions to even the most challenging problems.

Author Stephen Covey once said, "If you want to make minor, incremental changes and improvements, work on practices, behaviour or attitude. But if you want to make significant, quantum improvement, work on paradigms."

By actively seeking out new perspectives and being open to learning from others, we can challenge our flawed paradigms and make more informed decisions. Surrounding ourselves with positive influences and role models can also help us to shift our paradigms and adopt new ways of thinking that align with our true values and goals.

Ultimately, the way we see the world shapes the way we make decisions and take actions. By acknowledging our paradigms and being willing to shift them, we can make more informed decisions and take actions that align with our true purpose and fulfilment.

As the saying goes, "More is lost by the wrong paradigm than by a wrong decision." Let us choose to shift our paradigms and embrace a new way of seeing the world, so that we can live a life of purpose, meaning and fulfilment. It's not our decisions that lead us astray, but our flawed paradigms. By constantly examining and challenging our paradigms, we can make more conscious decisions and take purposeful actions. We can learn from the lions and adapt to new situations, rather than being bound by our old ways of thinking.

Bonus poem

Flawed paradigms can blind us to the truth,
And lead us down a path that's not so smooth.
Our decisions then become misguided,
And the consequences, often one-sided.

It's up to us to break free from this trap,
To open our minds and embrace a new map.
We must challenge our beliefs and be willing to learn,
To let go of what's old and let new ideas burn.

For when we shift our paradigms to what's true,
We unlock our potential and all we can do.
Our decisions then become clear and sound,
And we're no longer lost, but truly found.

Chapter 23 – The Power of Perception

Our perception is not just limited to external circumstances, but also how we perceive ourselves. If we believe that we are capable of achieving greatness, we will work towards it with unwavering determination. But if we believe that we are not capable, we will limit ourselves and never reach our full potential.

The power of perception is a force to be reckoned with. It can shape our thoughts, our actions and ultimately, our destiny.

The power of perception lies in our ability to choose how we view the world. We can choose to see obstacles as insurmountable barriers or as opportunities to learn and grow. We can choose to see failure as a defeat or as a stepping stone towards success. We can choose to see others as competitors or as allies in our journey.

The way we see the world shapes our thoughts, beliefs and actions. Our perception is influenced by our experiences, values, culture and upbringing. It's not the external circumstances that determine our happiness or success, but how we choose to perceive them. As Anais Nin once said,

"We don't see things as they are; we see them as we are."

Our perception can be both empowering and limiting. It can lead us to opportunities or hold us back from achieving our goals. For example, two people can look at the same situation and see it differently. One may see a problem while the other sees an opportunity. The difference is in their perception.

Perception is like a lens through which we view the world. It can be shaped by our paradigm, which is a set of beliefs and assumptions that we hold about the world. Our paradigm can be influenced by our upbringing, education, culture, religion and personal experiences.

Perception and paradigm shift are essential concepts in understanding human behaviour and relationships. In his book "Men are from Mars, Women are from Venus," John Gray highlights how men and women have different perceptions and paradigms that affect their relationships. For instance, he explains that men are problem-solvers and tend to withdraw into their "cave" when faced with challenges. On the other hand, women seek emotional support and communication when dealing with problems.

However, both men and women can benefit from a paradigm shift that allows them to understand and appreciate each other's differences. In an interview with Anthony Roberts, Gray emphasises the importance of shifting from a "win-lose" mindset to a "win-win" approach in relationships. He also highlights the need to recognise and appreciate the different communication styles between men and women.

Gray add that women often communicate to express their feelings and share experiences, while men communicate to solve problems and provide solutions. By recognising these differences and shifting their paradigm, men and women can learn to communicate more effectively and develop stronger relationships.

Anthony Roberts shared his experience of how his marriage was on the brink of collapse because of his inability to understand his wife's perception. He felt that his wife was always nagging and complaining, but she felt unheard and unappreciated. Roberts came to realise that their challenges were not about right or wrong but rather about perception. He needed to shift his paradigm to understand his wife's viewpoint, communicate effectively and show appreciation for her efforts.

In other words, shifting his paradigm allowed him to see his wife's perception and needs more clearly. By doing so, he was able to communicate more effectively, appreciate her efforts and ultimately save his marriage.

Perception and paradigm shift are not only relevant to gender relationships but also to individual growth and development. Our perception of ourselves and the world around us can shape our thoughts, beliefs and actions. A paradigm shift allows us to see things differently, question our assumptions and beliefs and explore new possibilities. By embracing a growth mindset, we can learn from our experiences, challenge our limitations and achieve our full potential.

We have the power to change our perception and shift our paradigm. By changing the way we see things, we can change the way we think, feel and act. We can choose to see challenges as opportunities for growth, failures as lessons and setbacks as temporary.

The way we perceive the world can have a profound impact on our lives. It can determine our happiness, success and fulfilment. By changing our perception, we can change our life. So, let's learn to see the world in a new light and embrace the power of perception.

As we go through life, we are constantly shaping and reshaping our paradigms based on our experiences and interactions with others. The way we see the world is not set in stone; we have the power to change our perception and create a more positive and fulfilling reality. We must challenge ourselves to look beyond our immediate biases and consider other perspectives, whether it's in our personal relationships or in our professional lives.

Children provide a great example of the power of perception and how it can change over time with a change in paradigm. As infants, they view the world in a very simplistic manner, with everything being either good or bad, happy or sad. However, as they grow and experience more of the world, their perception begins to change. They start to see things from different perspectives, understand complex emotions and develop a sense of empathy. A young child may perceive the world as a place of wonder and endless possibilities, while an older child may become more aware of limitations and challenges.

However, children also have the ability to shift their paradigms and change their perception as they grow and learn. For instance, a child who used to be afraid of dogs may shift their perception after learning more about them and having positive interactions with friendly dogs. This shift in perception can lead to a paradigm shift, where the child now sees dogs as lovable companions rather than scary creatures.

As adults, we can also learn from this childlike ability to shift our paradigms and change our perception. We can challenge our beliefs and assumptions and seek to understand different perspectives. We can choose to see the world in a different light and embrace new opportunities and experiences.

In man and women relationships, for example, it's easy to fall into gender-based paradigms that can limit our understanding of each other. Men may perceive women as overly emotional or irrational, while women may perceive men as insensitive or lacking in empathy. However, these paradigms are often based on societal norms and stereotypes rather than individual experiences and personalities. By actively working to challenge these paradigms and open up lines of communication, we can create more meaningful and fulfilling relationships.

Ultimately, it's up to us to take control of our paradigms and use them to shape our lives in positive ways. As American writer Henry David Thoreau once said, "It's not what you look at that matters, it's what you see." By choosing to see the world through a positive and open-minded lens, we can overcome challenges, build strong relationships and achieve our goals.

Anais Nin once said, "We don't see things as they are; we see them as we are." By taking the time to examine our own perceptions and experiences, we can work to develop a more accurate and compassionate view of the world around us. This, in turn, can help us to build stronger and more meaningful relationships, both with ourselves and with others.

Bonus poem

Perception is a powerful thing,
It can make us feel like we're flying on wings,
Or it can bring us down, to the depths of despair,
Making us feel like we're going nowhere.

The way we see things can change our whole world,
For better or worse, it can unfurl,
A new way of thinking, a new way to be,
Or a way of life that we just can't see.

So let's embrace the power of perception,
And use it to our advantage, without deception,
For we hold the key to unlock our fate,
With the way we see, it's never too late.

Chapter 24 – Sheer Determination and Belief in Oneself

Don't watch the clock; do what it does. Keep going.. - Sam Levenson

It's not always easy, but with determination, we can turn our dreams into reality and make a positive impact on the world around us.

Marcus Aurelius once said, "If it is humanly possible, consider it to be within your reach." This simple yet profound statement encapsulates the idea that humans are capable of achieving great things if they set their minds to it. He was a Roman Emperor who reigned from 161 to 180 AD and was the last of the Five Good Emperors and known for his philosophical writings, particularly his work "Meditations". Aurelius was also a military leader who spent much of his reign fighting against foreign enemies, including the Parthian Empire in the east and Germanic tribes in the north.

Despite the challenges he faced, Aurelius was known for his calm and rational leadership style and his commitment to the well-being of his subjects. He is considered one of the most respected and admired leaders of the ancient world.

Seneca, a contemporary of Marcus Aurelius, expands Aurelius's ideas by stating that "the greatest blessings of mankind are within us and within our reach". These words remind us that the key to success lies within ourselves and that we have the power to achieve whatever we desire.

To fully embrace this philosophy, we need to undergo a paradigm shift in the way we view our lives. We must shift our focus from external factors such as wealth, status and material possessions, to internal factors such as self-awareness, personal growth and emotional intelligence. By doing so, we can tap into the potential that lies within us and unlock our true capabilities.

In essence, the combination of Marcus Aurelius and Seneca's ideas teaches us that we are capable of achieving anything that we set our minds to. We need to have the courage to believe in ourselves and the willingness to put in the hard work required to reach our goals. With this mindset, we can shift our paradigm and achieve great things in our lives.

There are several real-life examples from Marcus Aurelius's time that illustrate the philosophy he espoused. One such example is the life of Epictetus, a slave who rose to become one of the most influential philosophers of his time. Despite being born into slavery and enduring numerous hardships, Epictetus persevered and went on to teach philosophy to some of the most prominent figures of his day, including Emperor Hadrian.

Another example is that of the Roman emperor himself, Marcus Aurelius. He faced numerous challenges during his reign, including wars, natural disasters and political upheavals. Yet, he maintained a stoic philosophy and continued to rule with wisdom and compassion, even in the face of adversity. His ability to remain calm and rational in the midst of chaos is a testament to the power of the human mind and the philosophy of stoicism.

Seneca, too, embodied the philosophy he preached. Despite being exiled from Rome multiple times and facing numerous setbacks, he continued to write and teach philosophy until his death. His words and ideas continue to inspire people to this day.

There are numerous other contemporary examples of individuals who have demonstrated the philosophy of Marcus Aurelius through their own perseverance and determination. One such example is Dr. Mona Hanna-Attisha, a paediatrician who exposed the lead contamination crisis in Flint, Michigan. Despite facing pushback from government officials and initially being dismissed as an alarmist, Dr. Hanna-Attisha continued to speak out and advocate for the health of the children in Flint. Her efforts eventually led to widespread acknowledgement of the crisis and action being taken to address the issue.

Climbing Mount Everest has long been considered one of the greatest challenges in the world of mountaineering. The feat requires sheer determination, physical and mental strength and a willingness to push oneself to the limits. However, in recent years, we have also seen a paradigm shift in the way that people approach the challenge of climbing Everest.

One example of this shift is the story of Nirmal Purja, a former member of the British Special Forces who set out to break the record for climbing all 14 of the world's highest peaks in just seven months. Purja faced numerous challenges along the way, including navigating dangerous terrain and adverse weather conditions. However, he remained committed to his goal and pushed himself to the limit, ultimately breaking the previous record by more than six years.

Purja's achievement was remarkable not only for the record-breaking time in which he completed the challenge, but also for the way in which he approached the task. Rather than relying solely on his own strength and expertise, Purja worked collaboratively with other climbers, sharing resources and knowledge to help each other reach the summit. This shift in mindset, from individual achievement to collective effort, reflects a broader shift in the world of mountaineering towards a more collaborative and community-focused approach.

Purja's efforts inspired a generation of Africans to shift their paradigm and achieve the seemingly insurmountable feat of climbing Everest. For many years, mountaineering had been dominated by Western climbers, with few people of African descent attempting to summit the world's highest peaks.

However, in recent years, this paradigm has begun to shift. African climbers such as South African Saray Khumalo and Kenyan Jackson Biko have successfully reached the summit of Mount Everest, inspiring a new generation of African climbers and challenging the notion that mountaineering is only for the privileged few.

The success of these African climbers highlights the power of sheer determination in overcoming obstacles and achieving one's goals. Despite facing numerous challenges, including the high altitude, harsh weather conditions and a lack of resources, these climbers persevered and ultimately succeeded in reaching the summit of Everest.

A story is told of a young Tanzania boy, Jabari, who had a dream in his heart and a vision in his mind. He wanted to sail the world, explore new lands and discover the unknown. But he had no ship, no crew and no experience. All he had was a burning desire to achieve greatness and a belief in his own abilities.

Jabari came from a small village by the sea in an area called Bagamoyo. His parents were poor fishermen and they had always told him to be content with what he had. But Jabari was different. He had a hunger for more, a thirst for adventure. He knew that he was destined for something greater and he was determined to make it happen.

He had read about the great explorers like Richard Francis Burton, who is credited with the discovery of Lake Tanganyika in 1858, one of the largest and deepest freshwater lakes in the world and Henry Morton Stanley, who explored the region around Lake Victoria in the 1870s and helped to establish trade routes and colonial settlements.

Jabari admired Soud Bin Soud, who was the first African to circumnavigate the African continent by sailboat in the 1970s and Bernhard Grzimek, who explored Tanzania's wildlife and natural habitats in the mid-20th century and was instrumental in the creation of Tanzania's national parks.

He had studied their journeys, their struggles and their triumphs. He knew that they had faced countless obstacles, but they had never given up. They had believed in themselves, in their abilities and in their dreams. He imagined himself sailing the world, crossing oceans and conquering new lands. He knew that it wouldn't be easy, but he was willing to do whatever it takes. He made a promise to himself that he would never give up, never surrender and never lose faith in his own abilities.

Years passed and Jabari worked hard to make his dream a reality. He saved every penny he earned and set sail with ten other like-minded Tanzanians on a journey that would change their lives forever. They faced storms, hunger and disease, encountered hostile natives, treacherous waters and unknown dangers. But they never gave up. They persevered, worked together and believed in themselves. They discovered new lands, mapped uncharted territories and made history.

After many years, Jabari returned to his village as a hero. He had achieved his dream and he had proved to the world that anything is possible if you have sheer determination, perseverance and a belief in your own abilities. He inspired a generation of young dreamers and he left a legacy that would never be forgotten in Tanzania and across the African continent.

The moral of the story is that no matter what your dream is, no matter how big or how impossible it may seem, you can achieve it if you have the power of sheer determination, perseverance and a belief in your own abilities.

These stories illustrate the importance of embracing new approaches and paradigms, as well as working together with others to achieve shared goals. Moreover, they demonstrate the philosophy of Marcus Aurelius, highlighting the power of sheer determination, perseverance and a belief in one's own abilities to achieve greatness. You have the power to transform your mind and create a brighter future for yourself.

Bonus poem

She stood before the mountain tall,
And felt so small, so very small,
Yet in her heart, a fire burned,
A flame of will that fiercely yearned.

She knew it would take more than might,
More than just muscle, grit and fight,
But a belief that she could do,
What others thought impossible too.

And so with sheer determination,
She started on her long ascension,
Step by step, she climbed up high,
Her strength and spirit never to die.

And as she reached the mountain's peak,
Her heart burst forth in joy and peak,
For she knew deep within her soul,
That with belief, she could reach her goal.

Chapter 25 – The Beauty of Our Choices

If your choices are beautiful, so too will you be. - Epictetus

Every decision we make, no matter how small, has the potential to influence the course of our lives.

Let's embrace the beauty of our choices, let's make them wisely and with intention and let's use them to create a life that we're proud of and a world that we're grateful to be a part of.

Epictetus, the renowned Stoic philosopher, once said, "If your choices are beautiful, so too will you be." His words are a powerful reminder that our choices have a profound impact on our lives and the person we become.

Every day, we are faced with choices. - some big, some small. Some have immediate consequences, while others have far-reaching implications that may not become apparent for years. It's easy to fall into the trap of thinking that our choices don't matter, that we can make them without much thought or consideration. But the truth is, our choices shape our lives in profound ways.

When we make choices that are aligned with our values that reflect the kind of person we want to be, we become more beautiful. We radiate an inner glow that comes from knowing we are living in harmony with ourselves and the world around us. When we make choices that are selfish, that go against our values, we become less beautiful. We may still have physical attractiveness, but it is overshadowed by an inner darkness that can't be disguised.

Consider the story of Malaika, a young woman from a small village in Venezuela. Malaika grew up with a strong sense of community, a deep respect for nature and a desire to make a positive difference in the world. She could have pursued a career in the city, chasing after money and material possessions. But instead, she chose to stay in her village, using her skills to teach children, tend to the sick and elderly and promote sustainable living practices.

Years went by and Malaika's choices led to a life of meaning and purpose. She was respected by her community, loved by her family and friends and had a deep sense of inner peace. Her beauty shone from within, radiating outwards and inspiring others to live a life of beauty, too.

Epictetus's words remind us that our choices are not just a matter of preference or convenience. They are a reflection of who we are and who we want to be. When we make beautiful choices, we become beautiful people. We attract positivity, joy and abundance into our lives. We inspire others to do the same. But when we make choices that are destructive, we become less beautiful. We invite negativity, despair and scarcity into our lives.

The power to choose is one of the greatest gifts we have as human beings. It's a responsibility that we should take seriously. Each choice we make is an opportunity to create something beautiful, something that will make us and the world around us more beautiful.

One of the key factors that have allowed humans to thrive is their ability to choose and shift their paradigm. However, paradigms are not fixed or immutable. They can change over time as new information and experiences challenge our existing beliefs and assumptions. At that point, we make other choices. This ability to shift paradigms is a powerful tool that can enable us to adapt to changing circumstances, overcome obstacles and create a better future.

A young Jamaican woman named Aisha came to the UK in 1998 and had many challenges adjusting to the life in the country. She felt stuck in her life. She had a job she didn't enjoy, was in a relationship that wasn't fulfilling and felt like she was just going through the motions each day.

One day, while on a walk in the park, Aisha had an epiphany. She realised that she had the power to choose how she thought, felt and acted and that this power could help her shift her paradigm and take control of her life.

Aisha began to reflect on her values, passions and dreams and realised that she wanted to start her own business. However, she had always believed that starting a business was too risky and that she didn't have the skills or resources to make it happen.

But now, with her newfound understanding of the power to choose, Aisha decided to take a leap of faith. She started researching business ideas and reaching out to potential mentors and investors. She also started to shift her mindset, replacing her doubts and fears with a belief in her own abilities and potential.

Despite setbacks and challenges along the way, Aisha persisted. She took courses, networked with other entrepreneurs and worked tirelessly to turn her vision into a reality. And eventually, her hard work paid off. She launched a successful healthcare business that aligned with her values and passions and that made a positive impact on the world. Today she employs over 300 people and has built a multimillion dollar business.

Reflecting on her journey, Aisha realised that the power to choose and shift paradigms had been the key to her success. By recognising that she had a choice in how she thought, felt and acted, she had been able to break free from her limiting beliefs and create the kind of world she wanted to live in.

Aisha's story serves as an inspiration to all of us. We all have the power to choose and shift paradigms, no matter where we are in life or what challenges we face. By recognising this power and using it to take control of our lives, we can create a brighter future for ourselves and for those around us.

The power to choose, therefore, is closely linked to the power to shift paradigms. When we recognise that we have a choice in how we think, feel and act, we can take control of our lives and create the kind of world we want to live in.

When we recognise that we have a choice in how we think, feel and act, we can take control of our lives and overcome even the most significant challenges. We can choose to be optimistic in the face of adversity, to be kind in the face of cruelty and to be courageous in the face of fear.

The power of choice also gives us the ability to shift paradigms. We can challenge our existing beliefs and assumptions, open our minds to new ideas and embrace new ways of thinking and living. With this power, we can create positive change in our lives and in the world around us.

Bonus poem

We hold within our grasp,
The power of choice at last,
To shape our lives and destiny,
And be all we were meant to be.

With every decision that we make,
A path to follow we create,
We can choose to take the road less trod,
Or stay on the beaten path, as is the norm.

Our choices determine our fate,
Whether we rise or meet our mate,
The beauty of our choices lies,
In the freedom to chart our own course and rise.

Chapter 26 – Overcome Limiting Beliefs & Create Wealth

Letting go of lack and embracing abundance opens doors to a life of prosperity and divine sustenance.

Open your mind, let old paradigms drift, abundance and wealth creation will come as a gift.

In today's world, riches and assets are within reach of those who actively pursue them. However, many people are still trapped in a scarcity mindset that prevents them from tapping into this abundance. They believe that there is only a limited amount of wealth available and that they have to compete with others to get their fair share.

This scarcity mindset can be deeply ingrained and difficult to break free from. But the key to unlocking abundance and wealth creation lies in shifting our paradigm. We need to let go of our old beliefs and ways of thinking that are holding us back and open our minds to new possibilities.

By changing our mindset, we can attract abundance into our lives. We can start to see opportunities that were previously invisible to us and take advantage of them. We can also cultivate a sense of gratitude for the wealth and abundance that we already have, which will attract even more abundance to us.

Wealth creation is not just about money, it's also about creating a life of purpose and fulfilment. When we shift our paradigm and tap into abundance, we can create a life that is aligned with our values and goals. We can pursue our passions and make a positive impact on the world.

So, if you're tired of struggling to make ends meet and feeling like there's never enough to go around, it's time to make a change. Open your mind, let go of old paradigms and embrace abundance and wealth creation as a gift that is available to us all. With a new perspective and a willingness to take action, you can create a life of abundance, purpose and joy.

Here is a simple lesson that is often misunderstood. There are two things you must know to create wealth. I think I'd be fairly safe in saying that at least 90% of everyone in this world wants to create wealth. And, if they've already got it, they want to create more, because it involves growth, going somewhere and doing something. What do you have to know? Just two things. Number one, you have to know where you are, you have to know where you're going and you've got to get moving. That is so simple and so obvious.

You have to ask yourself, why are so many people stuck?

The problem is where they are, their paradigm or set of ideas about money and the creation of wealth. They're being controlled by a paradigm that they don't know, they don't understand and yet it's keeping them right where they are.

Some of these people are very intelligent. They could have passed some very, very difficult exams in school, but they're stuck. They do not understand their paradigm. If you ask people what a paradigm is, most of them are at a loss to tell you. In fact, if you look up paradigm in the dictionary, you're going to find answers coming from very intelligent people, including behavioural scientists and psychologists, who explain it in very complicated ways.

And yet, it's just a group of habits in the subconscious mind that's controlling our behaviour. You know how to do better, but you're not doing it and you don't know why.

When asked about our beliefs and attitudes towards money, many of us may struggle to pinpoint exactly where they come from. However, the story of Wendy and her son serves as a powerful reminder of the impact that our programming and conditioning can have on our relationship with wealth. Wendy recognised that she had inadvertently passed on limiting beliefs to her son, which were preventing him from achieving financial success. This realisation led her to attend a seminar on the "Science of Getting Rich" with her son in tow, in the hope of shifting their mindset and creating new possibilities for their financial future.

Wendy's story highlights the importance of taking a critical look at our own beliefs and attitudes towards money. Often, these beliefs have been passed down to us from our parents, teachers and society at large and may be limiting our potential for wealth creation. However, as Wendy shows us, it is never too late to make a change. By attending seminars and seeking out new knowledge and perspectives, we can break free from old programming and open ourselves up to the abundance and prosperity that is available to us.

Ultimately, our beliefs about money shape our entire relationship with wealth, from our earning potential to our spending habits and our ability to create financial freedom. By taking the time to examine our programming and shift our mindset, we can unlock new possibilities for our financial future and create a life of abundance and prosperity.

No matter how hard one works or how many hours are put in, if the paradigm does not shift, the results will remain unchanged, leaving even the most intelligent individuals feeling discouraged. While those who are not very bright may expect nothing better, those who do expect better and are giving it their all are left without results.

So, what is the problem? The paradigm.

"The Secret" by Rhonda Byrne, both the book and movie, had a profound impact on my life. I have lost count of how many times I have listened to the audio book and read the text. The book promotes the idea that positive thinking and visualisation can help individuals achieve their goals and desires, emphasising that one's thoughts and beliefs about money can impact their ability to attract wealth. By focusing on the abundance of wealth in the world and believing that they are worthy of receiving it, individuals can unlock their potential to attract wealth.

In addition, "The Secret" motivates its readers to take active steps towards their financial aspirations and to appreciate what they already possess. This helps them shift their attention from pessimistic thoughts and attitudes towards optimistic ones. Individuals must release their inhibitions concerning money and adopt positive ones that empower them. For instance, one should eliminate negative assertions like "Money doesn't grow on trees" or "Money is the root of all evil" and replace them with affirmations such as "I am prosperous" or "I am already wealthy."

Byrne explains that individuals can attract positive experiences into their lives by focusing on positive thoughts and feelings and manifest their desires into reality by visualising them, believing that it is already theirs and taking inspired action towards their goals, trusting that the universe will bring them what they desire.

Changing your mindset is vital if you want to create wealth. The paradigm shift from negative thoughts and beliefs to positive ones, as advocated in "The Secret," enables individuals to attract wealth and abundance into their lives.

It is important to note that wealth creation is not an overnight process and it requires hard work, determination and a positive mindset. By taking action towards your financial goals, adopting empowering beliefs and affirmations and visualising your desired outcomes, you can manifest your aspirations into reality. Remember, the power to create wealth lies within you and it starts with changing your mindset.

Bonus poem

The mind can be a prison,
Limiting us from our true vision.
Beliefs we hold can be a shackle,
Blocking our path to financial tackle.

To create wealth, we must break free,
From the limiting thoughts that we see.
We must believe in ourselves and our worth,
And take action to manifest the earth.

The universe is abundant and free,
And our minds hold the key.
We must let go of our fears and doubt,
And trust that the universe will help us out.

With determination and a positive mind,
We can leave our limiting beliefs behind.
We can create wealth and abundance galore,
And live the life that we've been yearning for.

Chapter 27 – Unlock Infinite Potential

A paradigm shift can spark a revolution within, breaking down barriers and letting new possibilities begin.

When we embrace a paradigm shift, we open ourselves to a universe of infinite gifts.

As humans, we have infinite potential. There is no one alive that can even guess at what we're capable of doing. I have found out that the only way to improve our level of understanding is through study. There is no other way. To deal with change in our fast-moving world, we must develop our higher faculties.

Einstein put it very well. He said, 'The intuitive mind is a sacred gift, the rational mind is an obedient servant.'

He added, "We have created a society that honours the servant and has forgotten the gift." But do you know what that gift is?

While most people live their lives through their basic senses, there are higher faculties such as perception. It is through this higher faculty that one person can see a business or situation so differently from another, despite being in the same line of work. The gift is the ability to access and utilise these higher faculties to see the world in a unique way.

Your perception is your point of view. Perception is that intellectual factor, memory is an intellectual factor. This is what separates us humans from the rest of the animal kingdom. All the little creatures on the planet are completely at home in their environment, they can blend in. Humans are the only creatures on the planet that are totally disoriented in their environment and that's because they have been given the mental and creative tools to create or alter our own environment.

Wayne Dyer put it very well when he said, "When you change the way you look at something, what you look at changes." That's perception and your paradigm controls your perception. Your paradigm controls how you look at things and that is very, very important.

Now, think, another intellectual factor is imagination. Hill said it's the most marvellous, miraculous, inconceivably powerful force the world has ever known. Imagination is a very real part. Your imagination will permit you to go into the future and bring the future into the present and then begin living that way. It is, without a question, a phenomenal tool.

Humans, however, have to learn to use these tools. We have reason and the ability to choose our own thoughts. General Victor Frankl spent the war years in the concentration camp. He said that there's one thing he learned, regardless of the intellectual or physical abuse he was subjected to: no one could cause him to think something he didn't want to think.

Reason is what makes us free. Reason gives us the ability to choose our own thinking. We don't have to accept what we hear coming from the TV, radio or from the newspapers. We don't have to accept any that we can think for ourselves.

We also have another intellectual factor called *intuition*.

I could walk by you and like that, I could tell you all kinds of things about yourself. Your intuitive factor is that mental faculty that enables you to tap into vibration, to pick up vibration and translate it in your mind. You can pick up other people's energy, we're all doing it. We can learn how to really tune in or into an effect.

Another intellectual factor is *will*. When Dr. Wernher von Braun was asked by John Kennedy, the president in the United States at the time, to build a rocket that would carry him into the moon and bring him back safely to earth, he answered him in five words: 'The will to do it.'

To get any star you're shooting at, you must have the *will* to do it. Will gives us the ability to concentrate, which increases the amplitude of vibration, making our energy much stronger.

These are phenomenal tools that we all possess. The key is to learn how to use them and when we do, our lives change, our paradigms shift. Reflect on the areas of your life that your paradigm has almost exclusive control over. It controls your perception, use of time, creativity, effectiveness, productivity and logic. *Your paradigm literally controls your life.*

Now, here's another thing. When someone joins our company, one of the first questions I ask is, "What's the most you've ever earned in a year?" I'm not concerned about the actual number, but I want to know where their mind is focused. Your ability to earn money is controlled by your paradigm, not the marketplace or the people you work with. Your income is determined by your paradigm, which sets the conditions for your consciousness.

When you change your paradigm, you break free from the box that surrounds you, giving you the ability to make things happen. When you make the decision to change your paradigm, you knock down the walls and create room for growth and change. It's a huge difference and the change will be permanent.

Now, imagine if you changed your paradigm with respect to how you use your time. For example, if you decide to wake up an hour earlier every day to study, your understanding will increase. Solomon, in the Book of Proverbs in the Old Testament of the

Bible, said, "And all you're getting, get understanding." The only way to develop understanding is through study and one hour a day adds up to 940 hours in a year.

Bonus poem

Within each of us lies infinite power,
A wellspring of potential waiting to flower.
But often we're held back by limiting beliefs,
And fail to achieve our heart's true relief.

To unlock our potential, we must first believe,
In ourselves and all we can achieve.
We must cultivate our higher faculties,
And learn to tap into our intuitive abilities.

With reason, imagination and intuition,
We can change our lives and our condition.
We must break free from our limiting paradigm,
And embrace a new way of living and being sublime.

Let us awaken to our true potential within,
And live a life that's bold, creative and driven.
For we are limitless beings, capable of so much,
And our potential, once unlocked, will be a powerful touch.

Chapter 28 – Epilogue: Shift That Paradigm

Unleash the power within and shape your own reality through the paradigm shift of your thoughts and beliefs.

Break free from the confines of your comfort zone and embrace the transformative potential that lies beyond.

In the depths of self-discovery and growth, find the courage to rewrite your story and create a legacy of limitless possibility.

Thank you for joining me on this journey towards creating a paradigm shift in your life. We've explored the power of our thoughts and beliefs, the importance of breaking out of our comfort zones and the potential for transformation that comes with adopting new ways of thinking.

Remember, creating a paradigm shift is not an easy task and it won't happen overnight. It requires patience, persistence and a willingness to take risks and challenge our assumptions. But with dedication and hard work, it's possible to create real change in our lives. I encourage you to continue on this path of self-discovery and growth. Keep taking small steps towards your goals and remember to celebrate your successes along the way. You have the power within you to achieve your dreams and live the life you've always wanted.

Throughout this book, we have explored the depths of our minds and discovered the power within us to shape our own reality. We have delved into the realms of purpose, fear, discipline, creativity, passion and possibility, each chapter guiding us closer to our true potential.

Now, as we stand at the crossroads of our personal growth, we realise that the journey does not end here. It is a lifelong commitment to continuous improvement and self-discovery. Our paradigm shift is not a destination, but a compass that will guide us towards the life of our dreams.

In the process of embracing this new mindset, we have learned that our perception shapes our reality. We have shattered limiting beliefs and built positive habits that propel us forward. We have harnessed the power of emotional banking, nurturing our relationships and creating a reservoir of support and love. We have seized the moment, recognising that the perfect time to change is always now.

Through sheer determination and unwavering belief in ourselves, we have overcome obstacles and created wealth, not only in material abundance but also in joy, fulfilment and inner peace. We have tapped into our infinite potential, unlocking the doors to success and personal growth that we once thought were closed.

As we embark on this remarkable journey, let us carry the lessons learned and the wisdom gained into every aspect of our lives. Let us remember that flawed paradigms lead to flawed decisions and it is our responsibility to challenge and reshape them. Let us embrace the beauty of our choices and the impact they have on our present and future.

This chapter may be an epilogue, but it marks the beginning of a new chapter in our lives, one where we continue to strive for greatness, embrace change and live a life aligned with our purpose. It is never too late to change our paradigm, to rewrite our story and to create a legacy that inspires others.

So, my dear fellow paradigm shifters, let us embark on this next phase of our journey with enthusiasm, resilience and a commitment to living a life that is authentically ours. Together, we will leave behind a world touched by our transformation and a legacy of possibility.

Thank you for joining me on this extraordinary voyage of self-discovery and empowerment. May your paradigm shift continue to guide you towards the limitless horizons of your dreams.

So go out there and push for a paradigm shift. Embrace the challenges, learn from your failures and never give up on your dreams. You've got the power to do this!